PORTRAIT OF

HAWAII

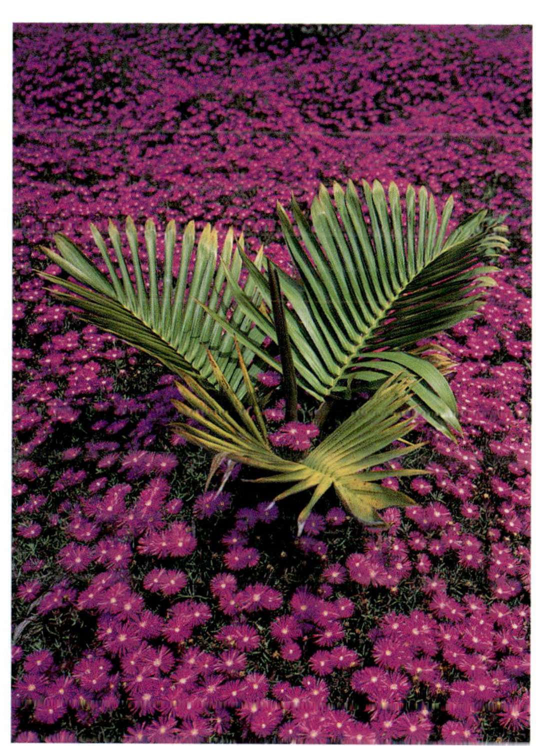

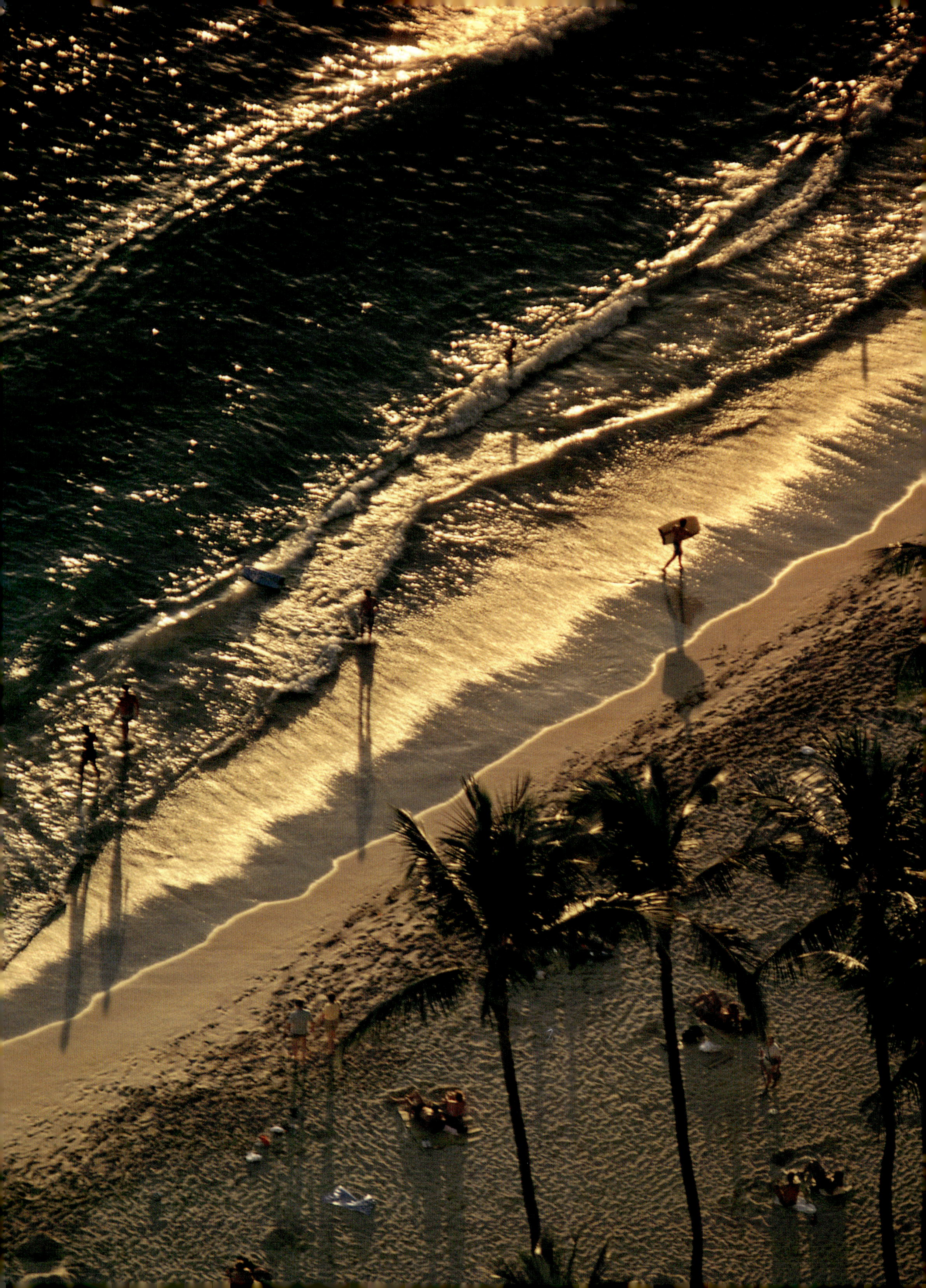

PORTRAIT OF

HAWAII

CLIFF & NANCY HOLLENBECK

GRAPHIC ARTS CENTER PUBLISHING®

Softbound ISBN 1-55868-527-8
Hardbound ISBN 1-55868-535-9
Library of Congress Catalog Number 99-76286

An imprint of Graphic Arts Center Publishing Company
P. O. Box 10306, Portland, Oregon 97296-0306
503/226-2402 — www.gacpc.com

President: Charles M. Hopkins
Editorial Staff: Douglas A. Pfeiffer, Ellen Harkins Wheat,
Timothy W. Frew, Alicia I. Paulson, Julia Warren
Production Staff: Richard L. Owsiany, Heather Hopkins
Designer: Jean Andrews
Cartographer: Manoa Mapworks
Book Manufacturing: Lincoln & Allen Company
Printed and bound in the United States of America

FRONT COVER: *Keikei hula,* or "children's hula," flourishes in the islands, as children learn the old language and customs. HALF TITLE PHOTO: A palm branch emerges among brilliant purple lampranthus blooms—called *akule kule* by Hawaiians. FRONTISPIECE: Surfers call it a day as Waikiki welcomes sunset. ▽ The colorful bird of paradise is a relative of the banana.

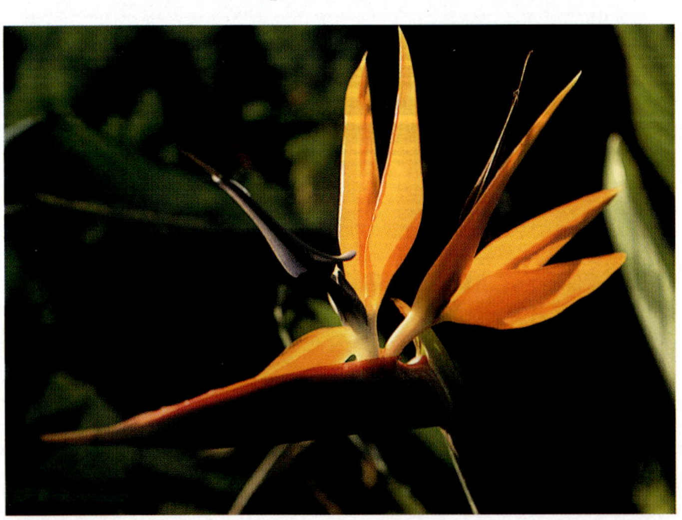

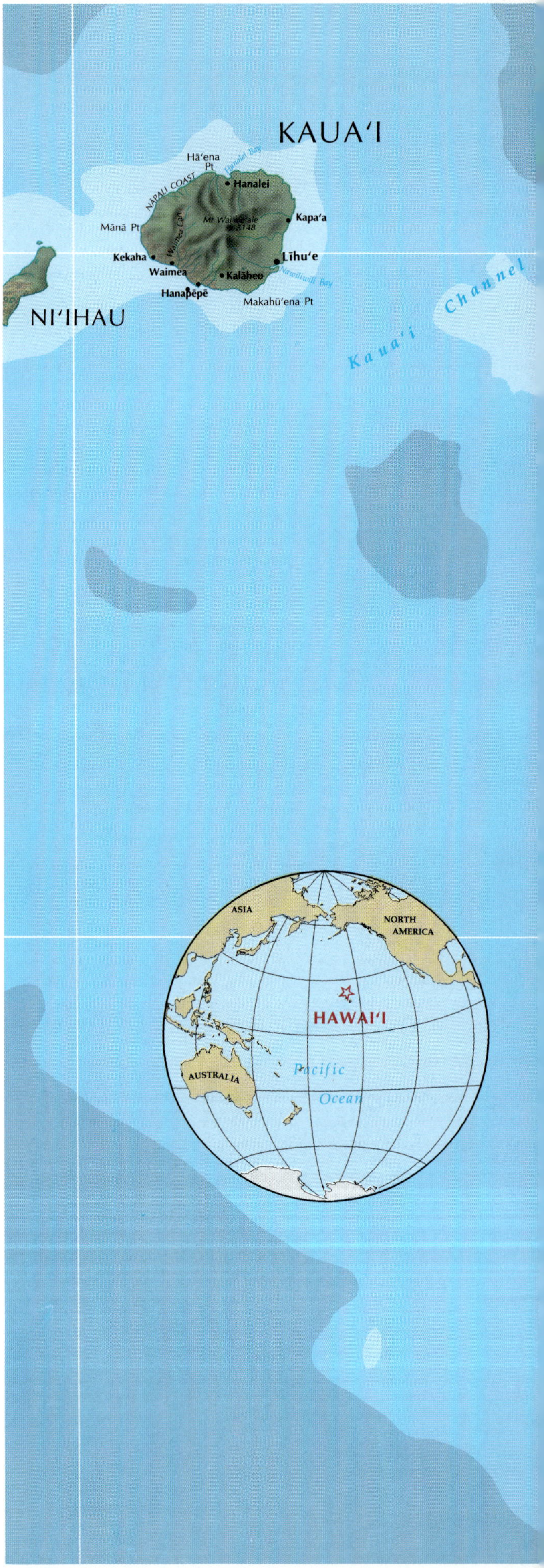

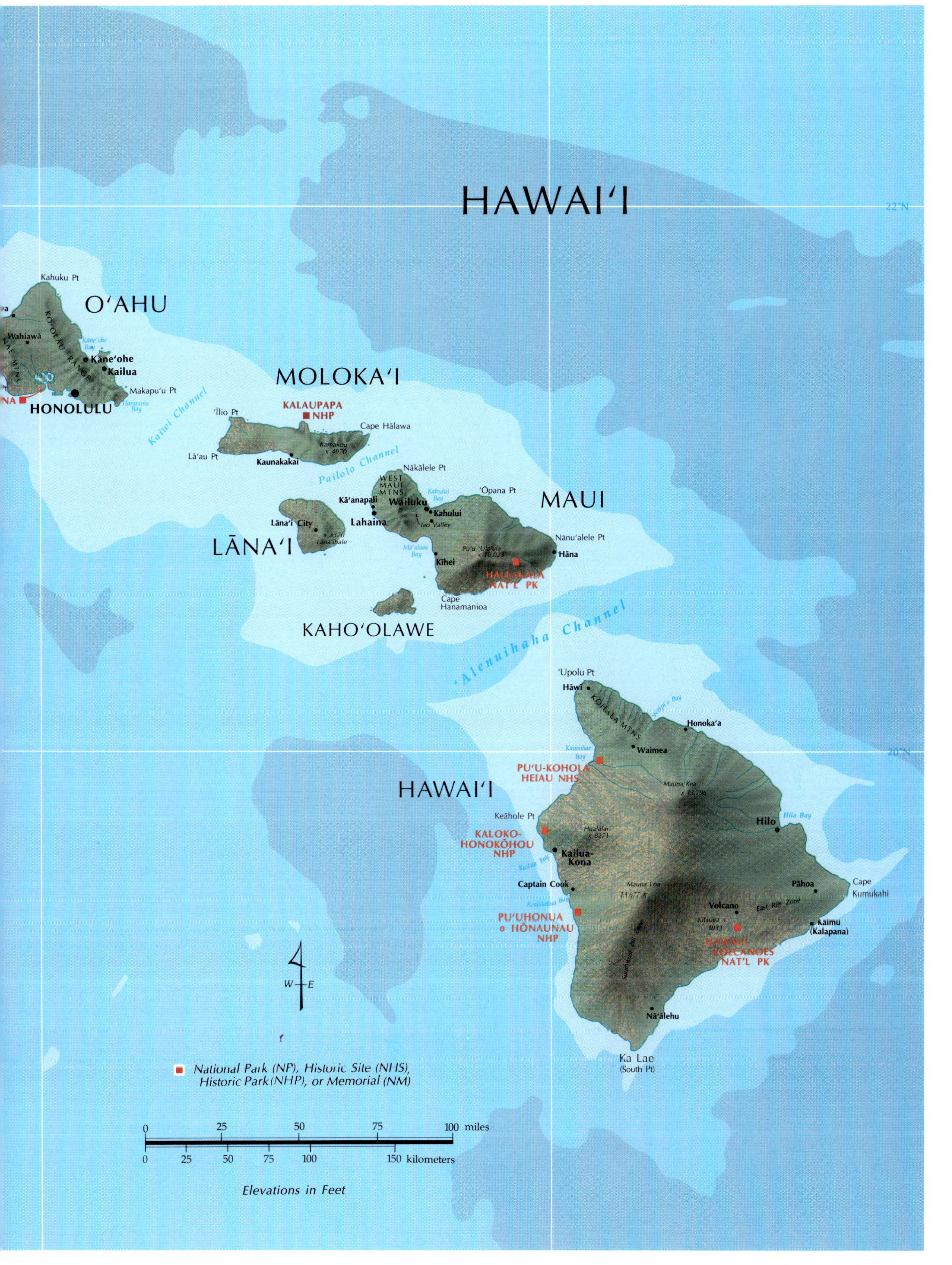

HAWAI'I
22°N
20°N
O'AHU
Kahuku Pt
Wahiawā
Kāne'ohe
Kailua
Makapu'u Pt
HONOLULU
Kaiwi Channel
MOLOKA'I
KALAUPAPA NHP
'Īlio Pt
Cape Hālawa
Lā'au Pt
Kaunakakai
Pailolo Channel
Nākālele Pt
WEST MAUI MTNS
Kā'anapali
Wailuku
Kahului
Lahaina
'Ōpana Pt
MAUI
Lāna'i City
LĀNA'I
Nānu'alele Pt
Hāna
Kīhei
HALEAKALĀ NAT'L PK
Cape Hanamanioa
KAHO'OLAWE
'Alenuihāhā Channel
'Upolu Pt
Hāwī
KOHALA MTNS
Honoka'a
Waimea
PU'U-KOHOLĀ HEIAU NHS
HAWAI'I
Keāhole Pt
KALOKO-HONOKŌHOU NHP
Hilo
Hilo Bay
Kailua-Kona
Captain Cook
Pāhoa
Cape Kumukahi
Volcano
Kaimu (Kalapana)
PU'UHONUA o HŌNAUNAU NHP
HAWAI'I VOLCANOES NAT'L PK
Nā'ālehu
Ka Lae (South Pt)
W
E
National Park (NP), Historic Site (NHS), Historic Park (NHP), or Memorial (NM)
0 25 50 75 100 miles
0 25 50 75 100 150 kilometers
Elevations in Feet

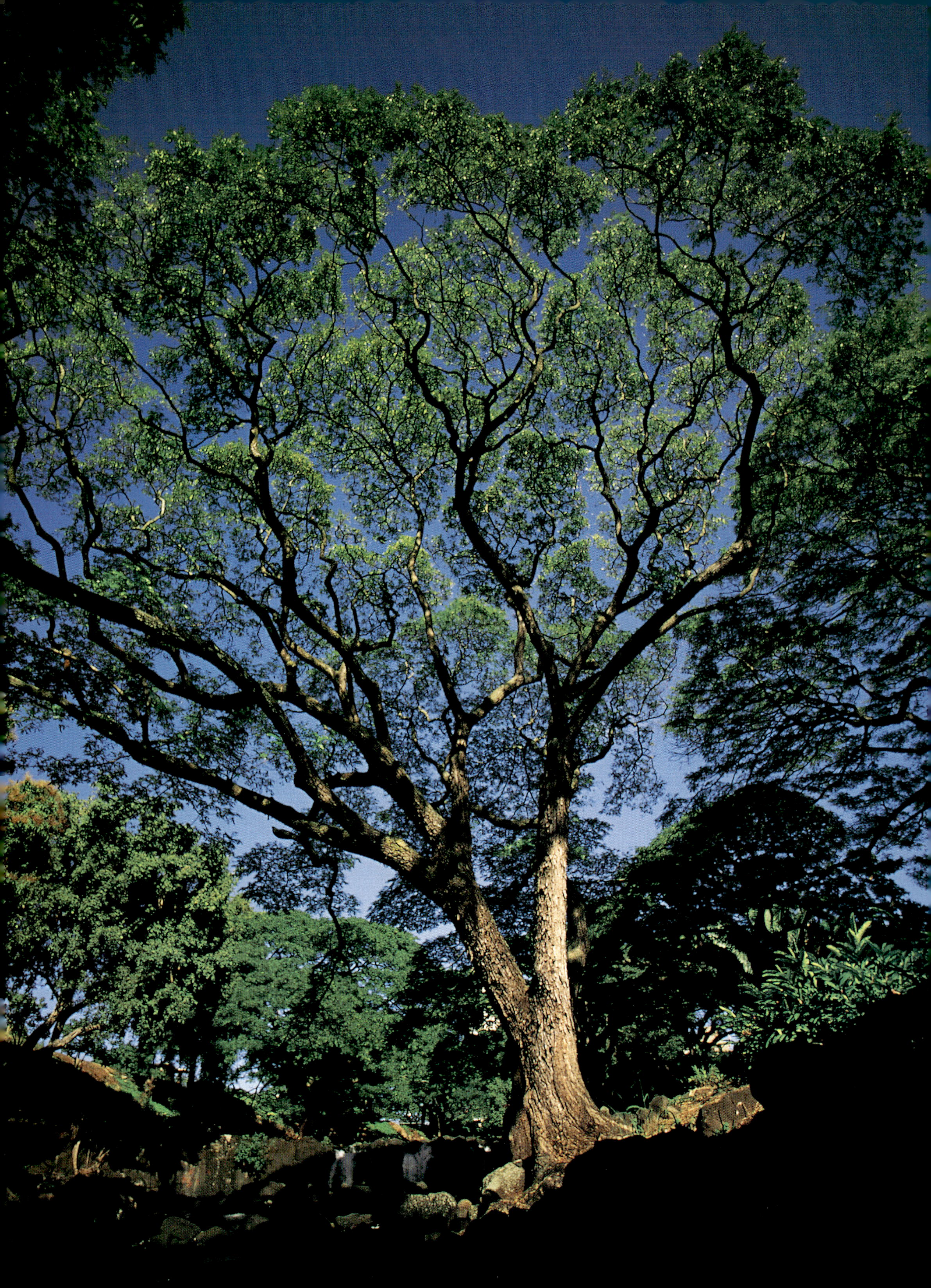

Overview

In double canoes they came, more than thirteen hundred years ago, searching northward into an unknown sea. Sailing on strange winds, paddling through doldrum calms, braving high seas and storms, they persisted in their quest for new land. . . . While other men sailed within the comforting presence of continental coasts, Polynesians faced the open sea without fear as their own and only world. Sailing now under the stars of the northern sky, reaching across powerful northeastern trade winds, they came upon a chain of Islands of tremendous size, far larger than any they had known. When their canoes touched sand Man's history in Hawaii had begun.

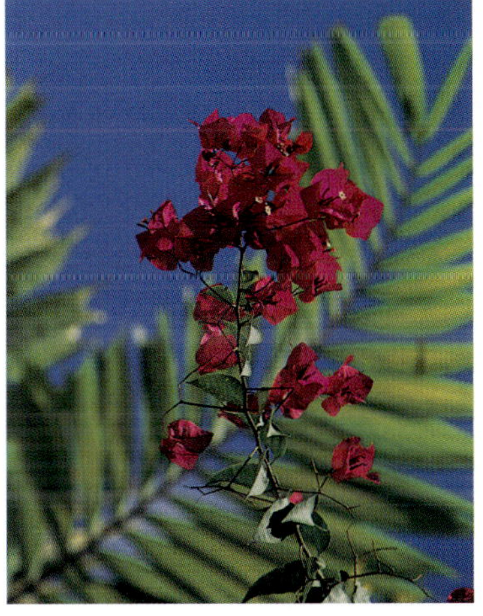

Through these words from the Prologue of *Voyage: The Discovery of Hawaii,* author and Living Hawaiian Treasure Herb Kawainui Kane describes the first Hawaiians and their quest for paradise.

Despite innumerable outside influences, two elements from that voyage of discovery have survived over hundreds of years: the *Ohana*'s spirit of *Aloha* and the incredible paradise those first Hawaiians discovered. The *Ohana* is generosity given without restraint or hidden purpose. Early Hawaiians had an ingrained custom: "We will share what we have with you, and you must share what you have with us." It still is the heart of the *Ohana.* Hawaiians call it *Aloha.* The most important word in the Hawaiian language, *Aloha* means dozens of things, including hello, welcome, greetings, good-bye, farewell, or I love you.

Each island was individually controlled by its own hierarchy of kings, chiefs, and nobles. Life, including food, marriage, work, gratification, and privilege, was subject to the *kapu,* or rules, and of course, the *Ohana.* The only higher authority, which was often interpreted by the royalty, came from their gods, which numbered more than two hundred.

Europeans were the first recorded outsiders to explore the islands and experience the spirit of *Aloha.* Captain James Cook's visit to Kauai's west coast in 1778 was the first of a series of events that would shape the islands, which had remained essentially the same since the Polynesians had landed a thousand years earlier. Cook named them the Sandwich Islands—after the Earl of Sandwich, his sponsor and the First Lord of the Admiralty—a name that endured into the next century.

Following their custom, the natives shared their exotic foods, balmy weather, beaches, and beautiful women with Captain Cook, a man they thought was a god, and his men. The Europeans, however, paid little attention to the native culture or rules of *kapu.* A year later, when Captain Cook visited the islands again, stopping at Kealakekua Bay on the Big Island, the locals quickly recognized that they had been wrong in thinking he was a god. Cook was killed during a dispute over missing property.

Ten years later, a warrior named Kamehameha began a decade-long campaign to unite the islands under his rule. Aided by advice from two English seamen who fired cannons mounted in his canoe, he successfully used European warfare technology to capture all the islands except Kauai. Because of the treacherous channel, attempts by his fleets to invade Kauai were thwarted. Turning to threats and diplomacy, Kamehameha eventually obtained Kauai's surrender to his rule, and all the islands became a united kingdom.

◁ *Located in downtown Honolulu, the Liliuokalani Botanical Garden provides tranquility in the midst of hectic city life.*
△ *Bougainvillea, a native of Brazil, brightens the islands throughout winter, spring, and early summer.*

The early 1820s were conceivably the most influential period in Hawaii's history. Following the death of Kamehameha the Great, the *kapu* system of governing was abolished. Then, as if in answer to the need for spiritual guidance, Christian missionaries arrived and immediately set about filling the void. They established a written Hawaiian language—enabling the Hawaiians to record their ancient oral histories—and introduced hymn singing to help teach their religion. Sadly, the missionaries also denounced bare skin, chants, and the ancient hulas, which were outlawed for many years.

During this time, the sandalwood trees were cut and traded into extinction, leaving the islands hungry for new economic resources. Again, fate stepped in with the business of whaling. Honolulu and Lahaina were among the world's most profitable ports. With whaling came liquor, prostitution, and disease. Missionaries spoke against these vices, but their admonitions fell on deaf ears. Even King Kamehameha III rebelled by drinking, gambling, and dancing the hula. In less than a generation, the whales began to disappear, and Hawaii was again hungry for a source of income.

Before outsiders arrived, Hawaii had no private land ownership. Everyone had access to all lands except those protected by royalty. King Kamehameha III opened up ownership of the land to all, but because the Hawaiians did not understand this concept, most of the land was acquired by businessmen, immigrants, and second-generation missionaries. Today, about half of Hawaii is government controlled. Three-quarters of the rest is held by fewer than forty owners.

Sugarcane and pineapple became big business. Because the native Hawaiians did not care for the hard work, the growers began to import laborers from China, later turning to Japan, the Philippines, Korea, and Portugal.

Hawaii entered the modern political world with the passing of King Kamehameha V, who left no direct heir to assume power. Prince Lunalilo was elected king, but he served only a year before he died. The resulting chaos brought strong calls for annexation to the United States. The calls went unheeded by the new King Kalakaua, who preferred his own government.

In 1887, Caucasian businessmen and missionary descendants led an armed uprising that forced the king to accept the "Bayonet Constitution," which allowed only land owners and well-employed men to vote. Political control shifted to the white minority.

King Kalakaua died during a visit to San Francisco in 1891, leaving Lydia Liliuokalani as Hawaii's first reigning queen. She attempted to restore the power of royalty and the rights lost by the native Hawaiians as a result of the Bayonet Constitution. A revolt ensued, and marines from a visiting gunship surrounded the royal palace. Without a single shot being fired, the monarchy was overthrown in 1893, and Sanford Dole (whose relative, James, later became pineapple king) took control of a provisional government.

Queen Liliuokalani's overthrow was illegal according to international law. President Cleveland attempted to correct this "illegal act against a foreign government," but Congress ignored him. In 1900, Hawaii became a U. S. territory, eliminating the royalty.

During the first half of the twentieth century, tourists began a new kind of takeover of the islands, until the bombing of Pearl Harbor shattered the serenity of this peaceful tropical getaway in 1941. Tourism would soon rebound, however, because the war introduced the islands to thousands of American military men who would later return as tourists.

World War II also brought more political and military attention to Hawaii. As senior United States military commanders and politicians began to visit Hawaii, they saw the islands as the new business gateway to Asia and the Pacific. Because Pearl Harbor was the single most important military base outside the United States, its bombing tied the islands to America forever. After the war, more than twenty legislative bills addressing the issue of U. S. statehood for Hawaii were considered by the American Congress. Despite the attention, it still took nearly fifteen years before the U. S. Congress offered Hawaii statehood. In 1959, in a deal that was linked with Alaska's statehood, Hawaii became the fiftieth state.

After World War II, government and agriculture were the most important economic factors in Hawaii's development. However, commercial jet service soon linked Hawaii with the U. S. mainland, Australia, and Asia—and tourism began to soar. Suddenly, people who wanted to see paradise for themselves could travel there in less time than it took to enjoy a meal and a movie. And travel they did.

Today, Hawaii is one of the world's most popular destinations. The islands are home to a diverse, yet harmonious society. Quality of life and average life expectancy is among the highest in the United States, while unemployment, violent crime, heart disease, and deaths from cancer are among the lowest. Hawaiians will tell you the reason has always been the *Ohana*, their spirit of *Aloha*.

△ *Lobster claw heliconia, native to tropical America, grows in clumps of paddle-shaped leaves, hiding its flowers inside bright red sheaths.*
▷ *Mokolii Island, better known as Chinaman's Hat, is a tiny island set off the windward side of Oahu.*

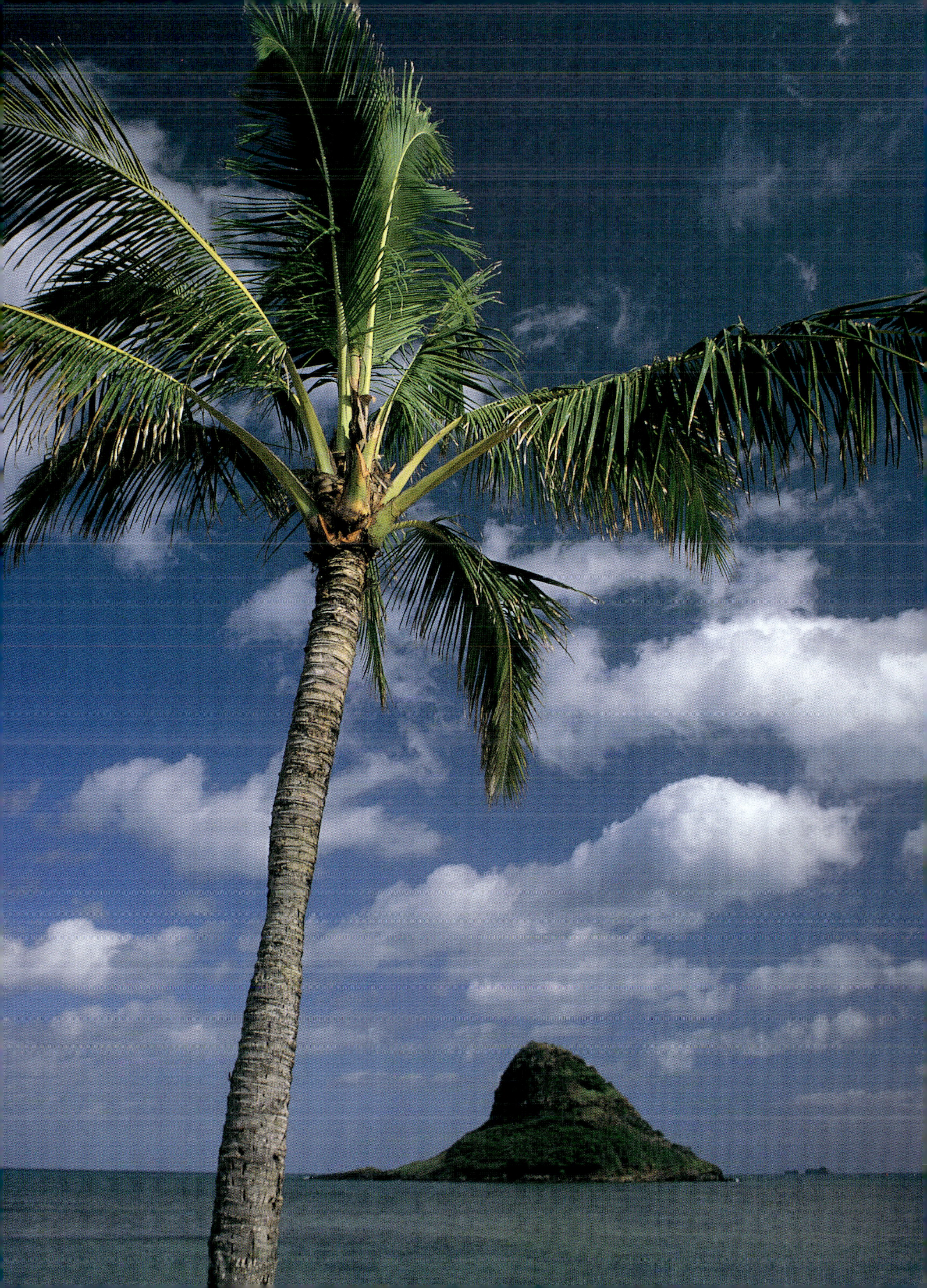

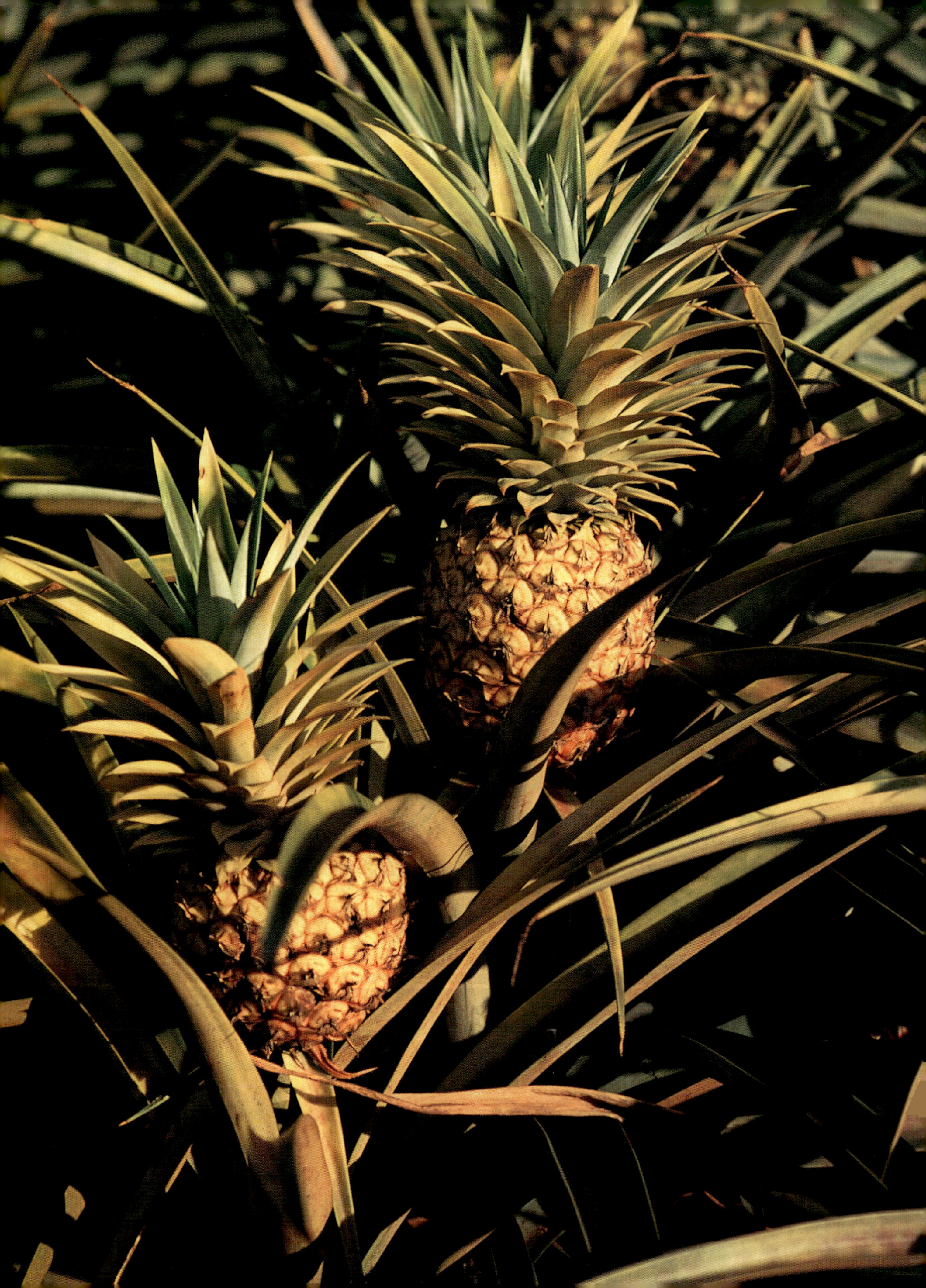

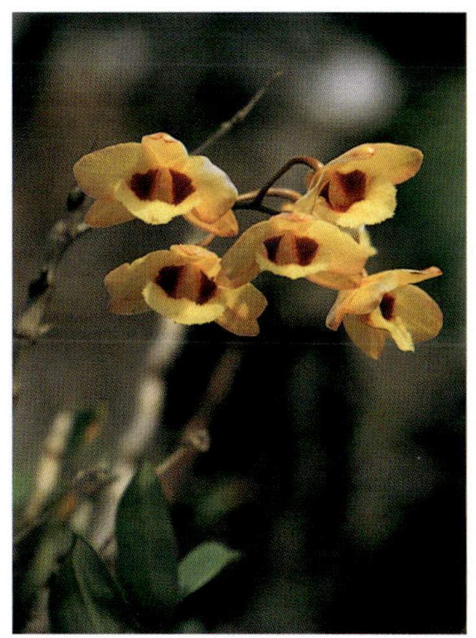

Oahu

Oahu has been the primary center of business, society, and culture since the Hawaiian Islands were united into a kingdom two centuries ago. The monarchy chose its main city of Honolulu for the Royal Palace. Following U. S. statehood, it became the capital. The first tourists docked here a hundred years ago, and today more than six million visitors pass through its international airport each year. More than 80 percent of Hawaii's population lives here, while occupying only 10 percent of the state's total land mass.

The perfect natural harbor that early Hawaiians named *Honolulu*, or "Protected Bay," is the only sheltered harbor within two thousand nautical miles, making it the business and shipping gateway between the South Pacific, Asia, and America. Nearby Pearl Harbor, made navigable a hundred years ago, houses one of the most strategic military bases outside the continental United States. It is also the site of the Arizona Memorial, a tribute anchored over the battleship USS *Arizona,* sunk by the Japanese on December 7, 1941.

Oahu is also called the "Gathering Place," for it is home to the most diverse group of ethnic peoples of any municipality in the world. It is not an uncommon day to hear words spoken in Hawaiian, Chinese, Japanese, Korean, Thai, Portuguese, several Pacific Island languages, and English. Each of these civilizations has contributed to the rainbow culture that is modern Hawaii.

◁ *A wide stretch of pineapple fields occupies much of central Oahu.*
△ *Dendrobium is among some 700 orchid species in the islands.*
▷ ▷ *A replica of Japan's Byoto-In Temple lies in Valley of the Temples.*

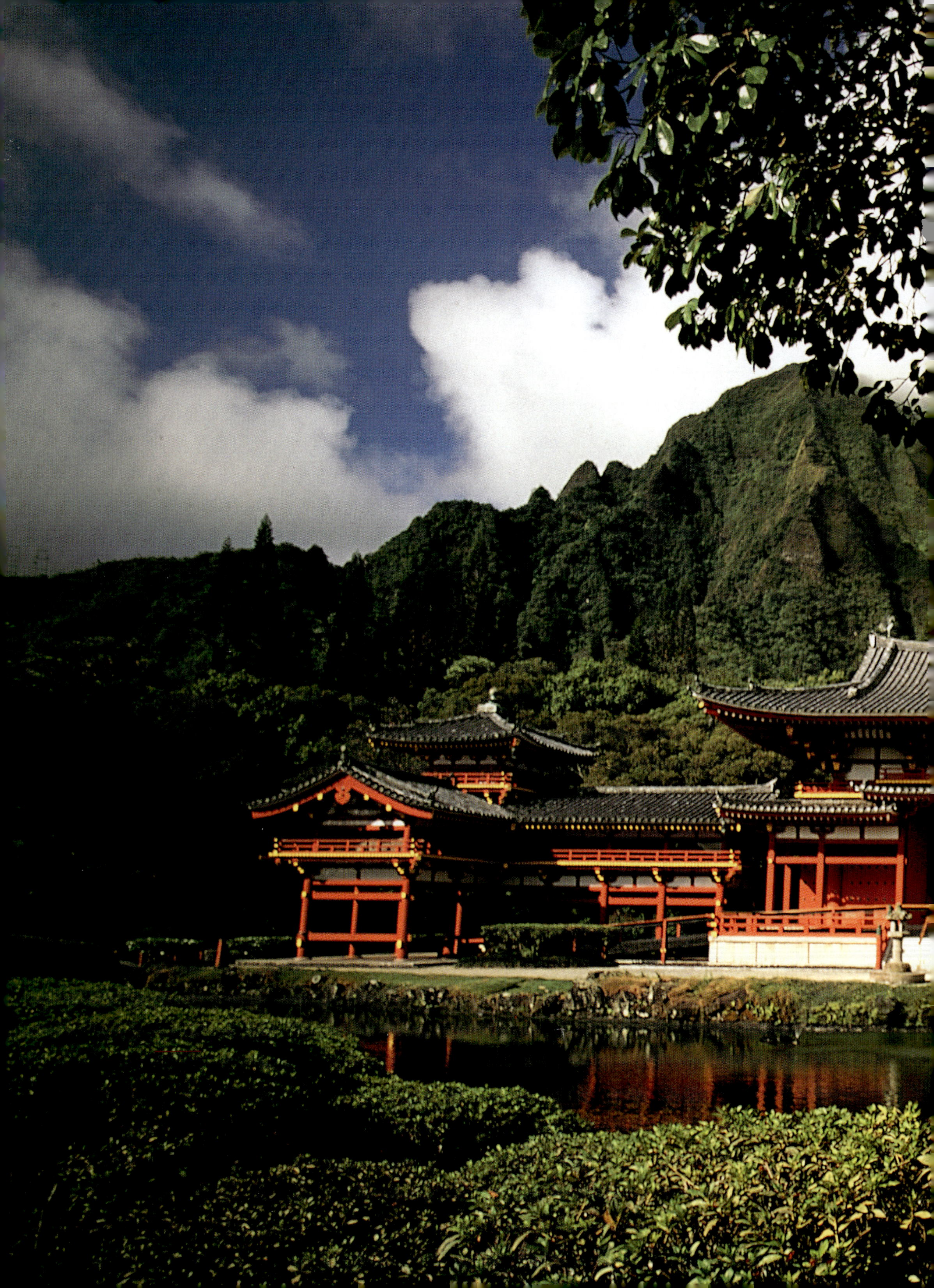

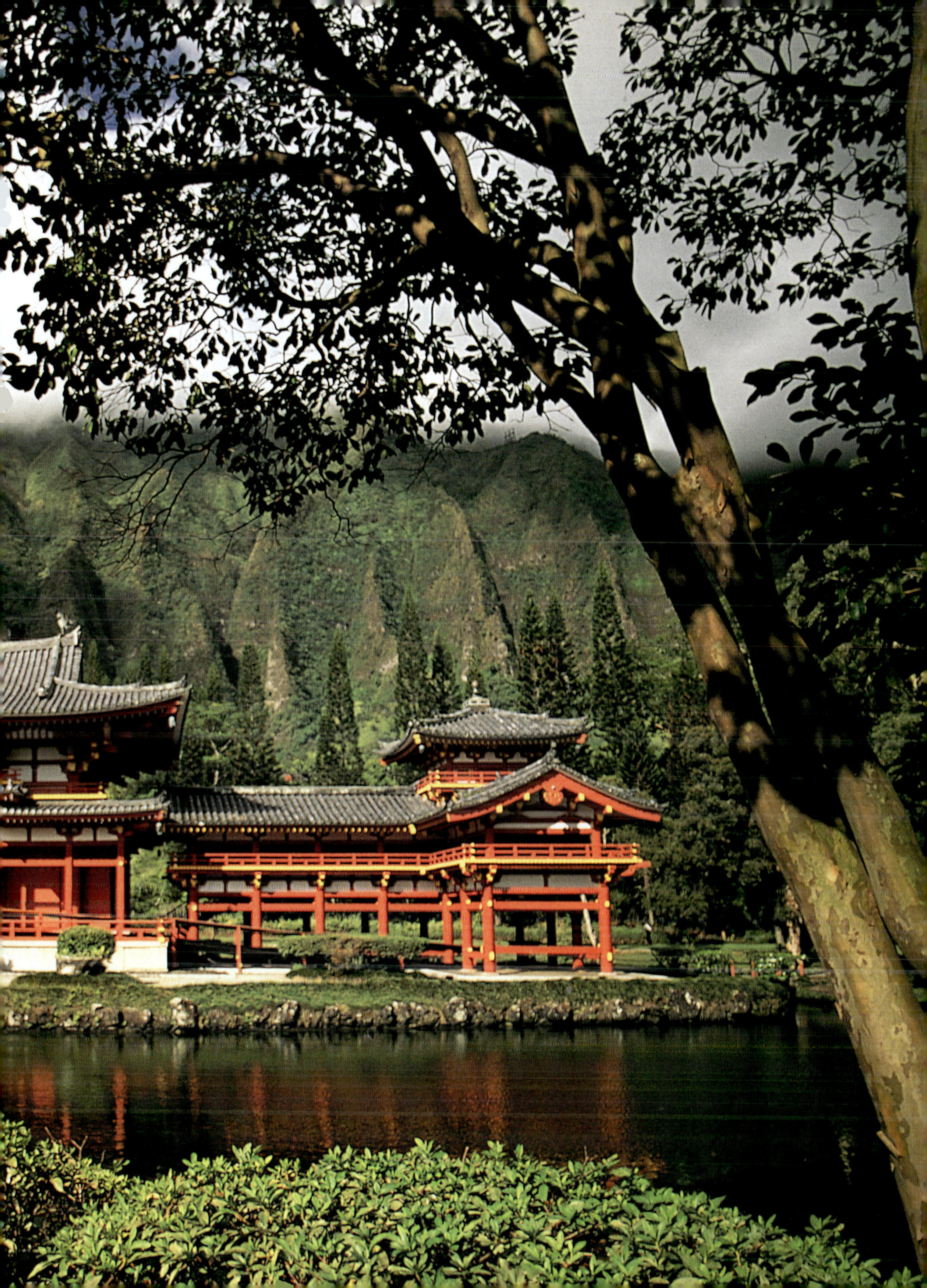

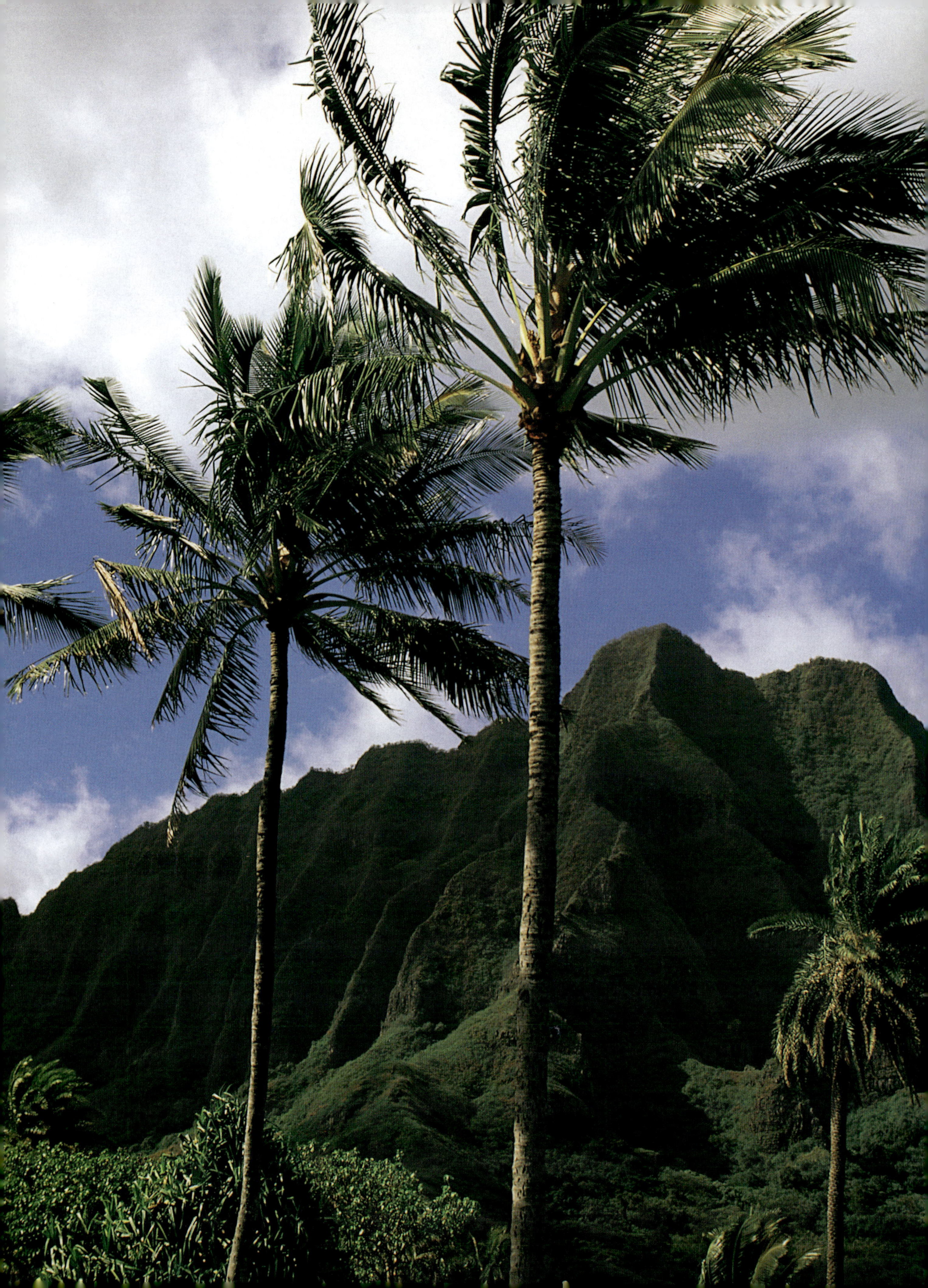

◁ From Makapuu to the North Shore of Oahu, the towering Koolau mountain range is home to crystal waterfalls, green valleys, and rugged cliffsides. ▽ A Polynesian couple from Tonga grow fruit at their home and sell it at this stand along the North Shore road. Locals from a multitude of ethnic backgrounds sell food or their homemade crafts at stands throughout the islands.

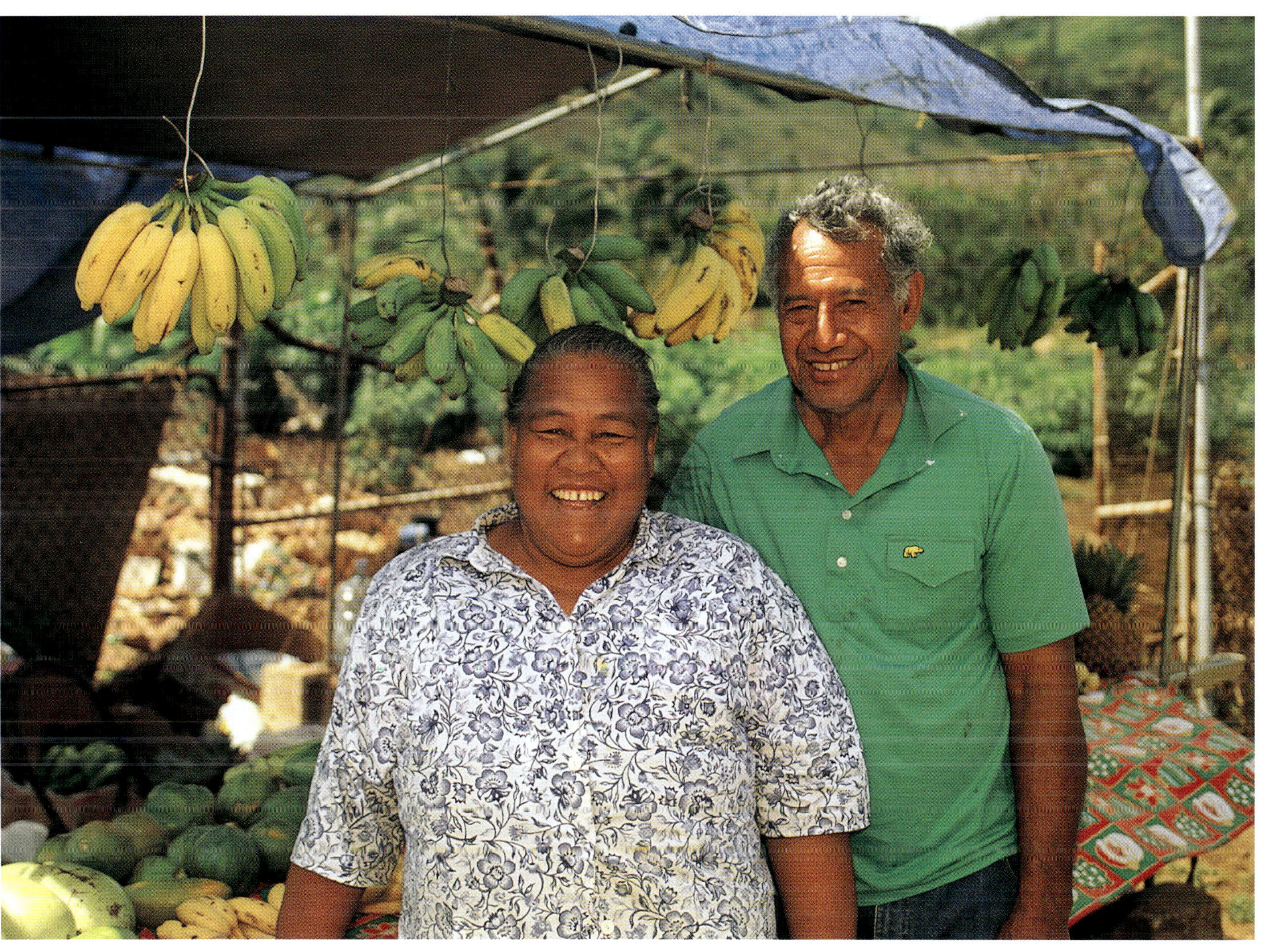

▽ Of the USS *Arizona*'s original crew of 1,012 men, more than 900 are believed to be at rest with the remains of the ship at the bottom of Pearl Harbor. The simple, stark white Arizona Memorial pays moving homage to those who lost their lives on December 7, 1941, when Japanese dive bombers sank the U. S. Pacific Fleet at anchor. ▷ Spectacular Waikiki Beach, with Diamond Head rising majestically behind, was a playground for the Hawaiian monarchy long before the building boom of the 1950s turned the area into one of the most visited spots on earth.

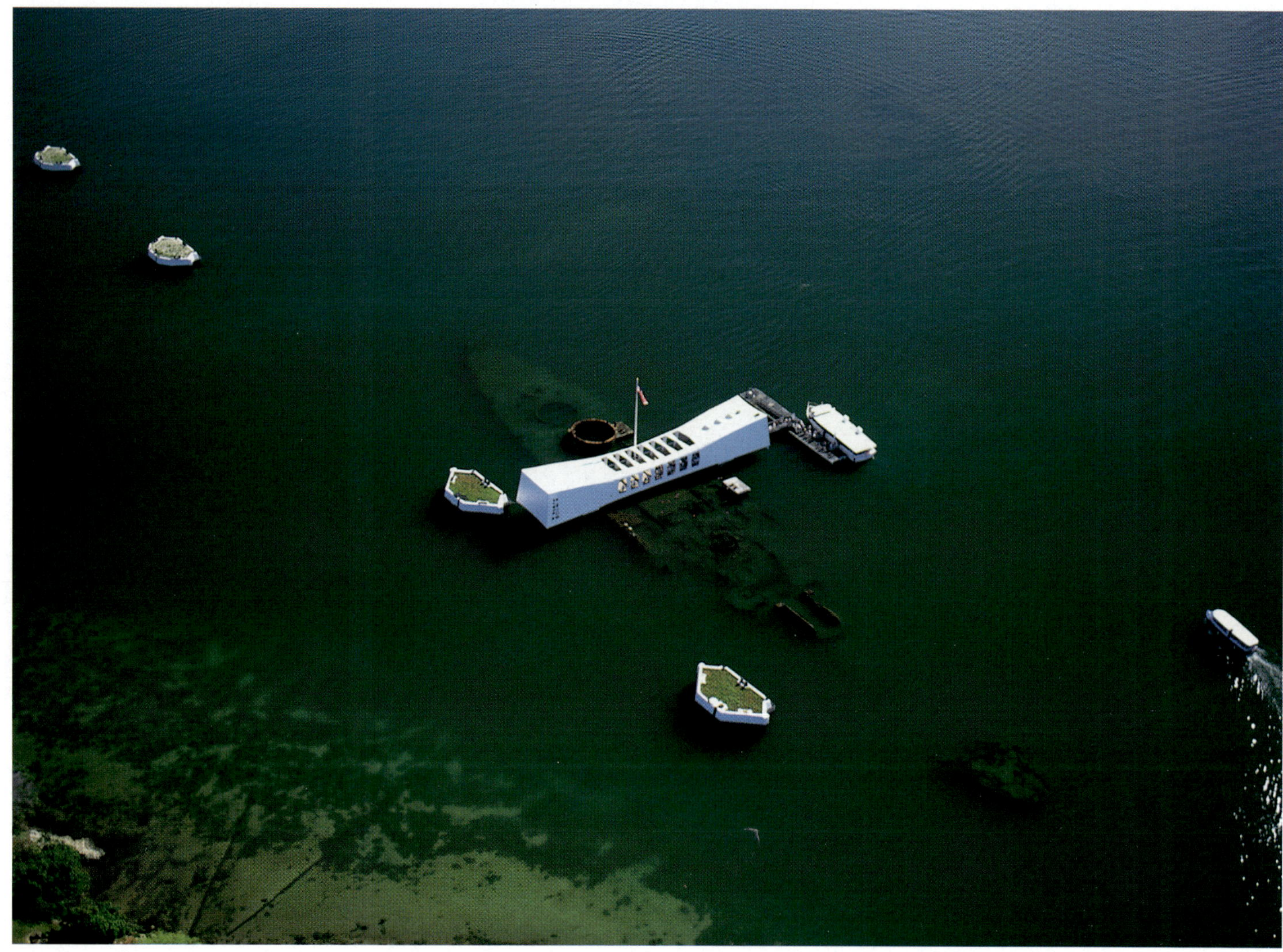

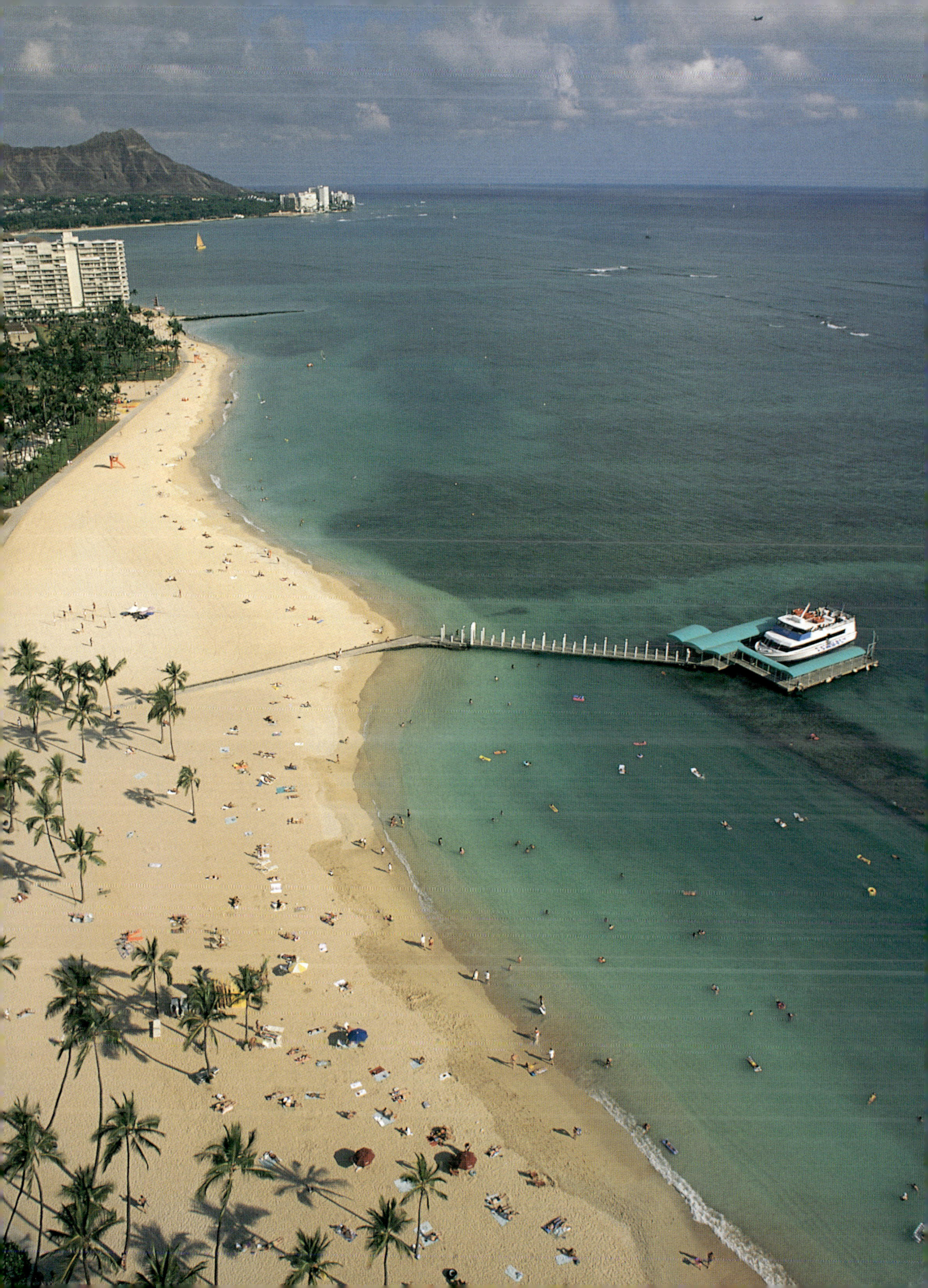

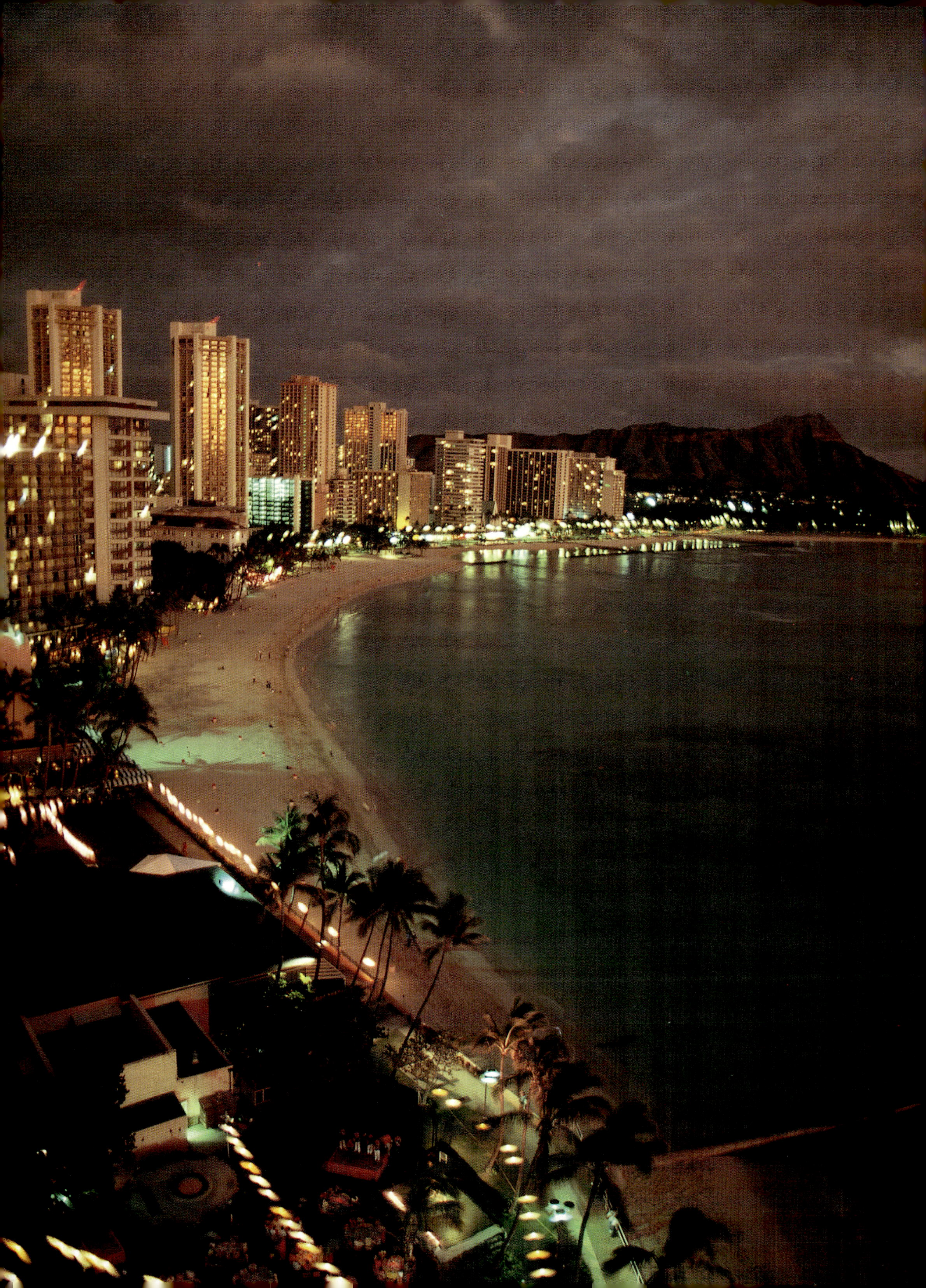

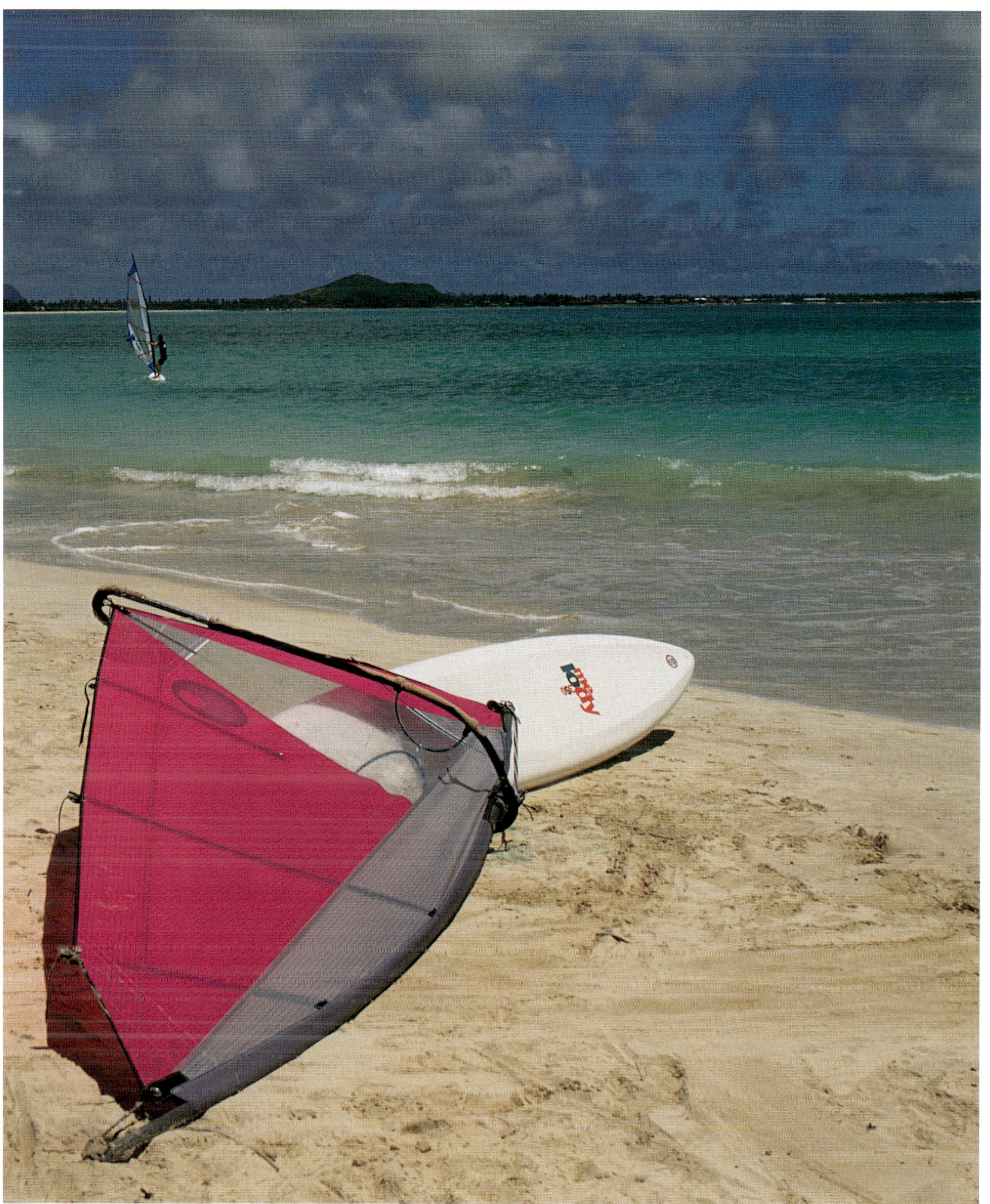

◁ At night, myriad lights glow along the famous one-and-one-half-mile crescent of sand known as Waikiki Beach.
△ Set along Kailua's windward coast, beautiful Lanikai Beach is a favorite spot for sailing and windsurfing.
▷ ▷ Coral formations teaming with fish are visible beneath the brilliant emerald blue waters of Hanauma Bay.

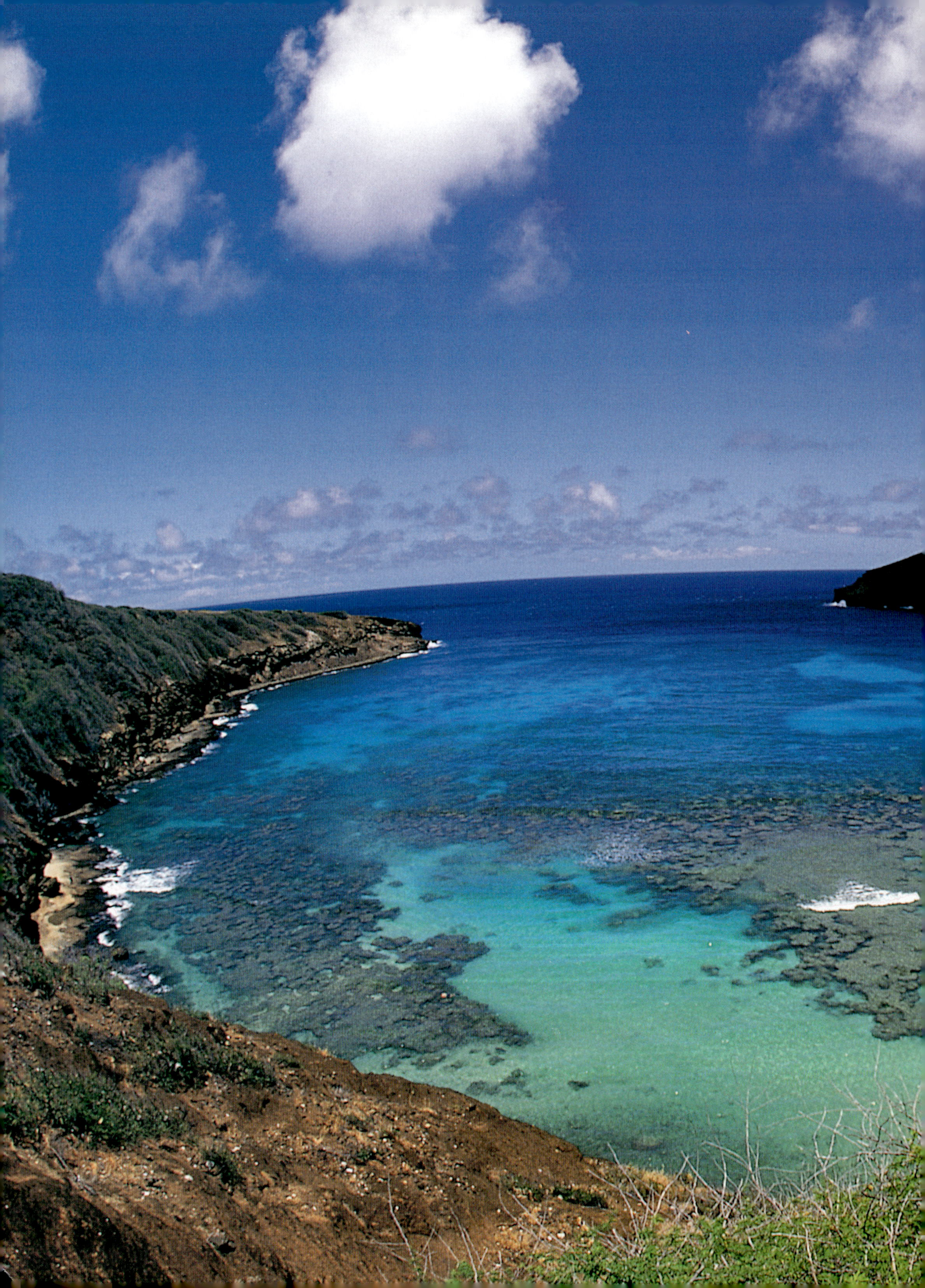

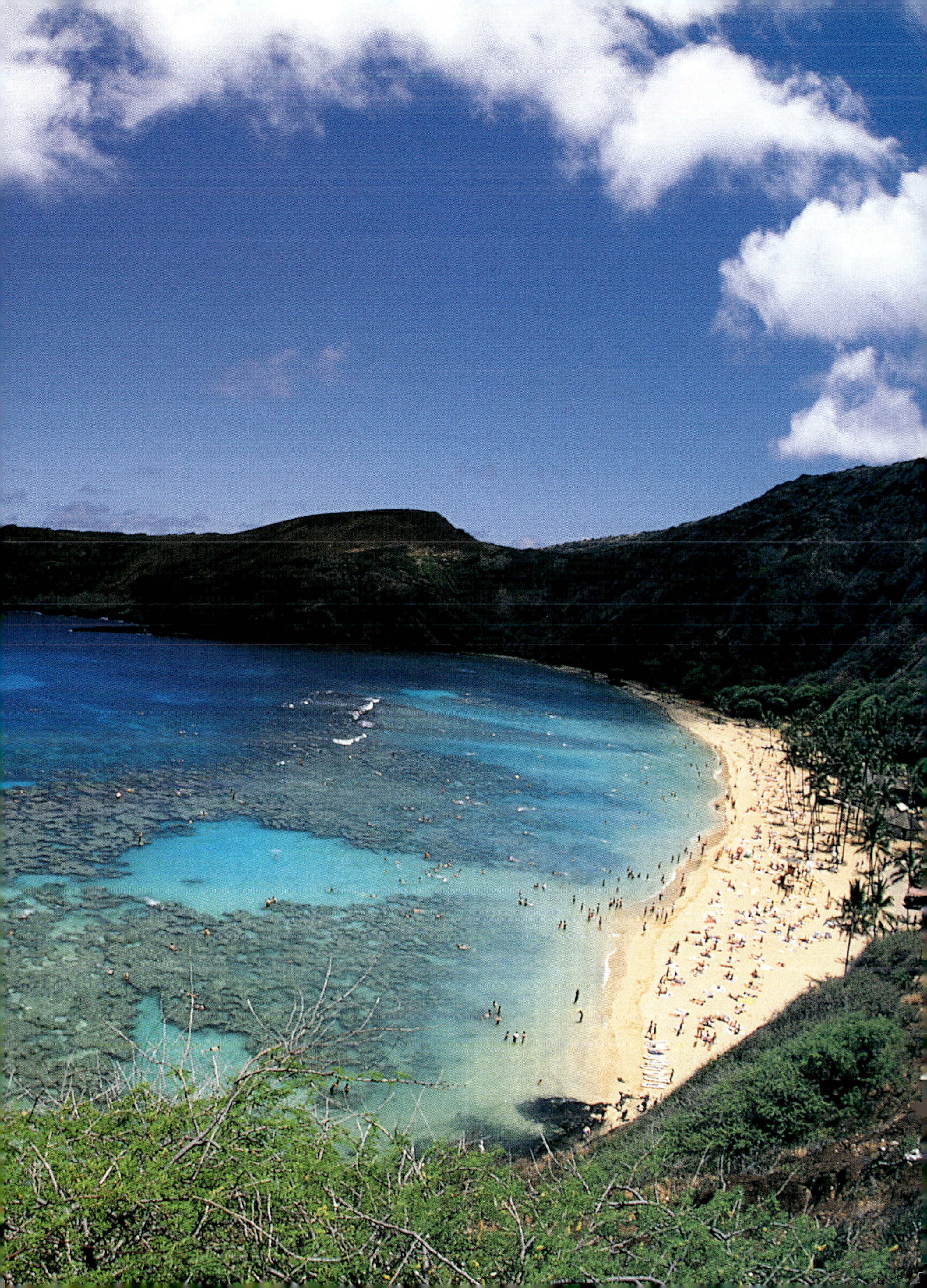

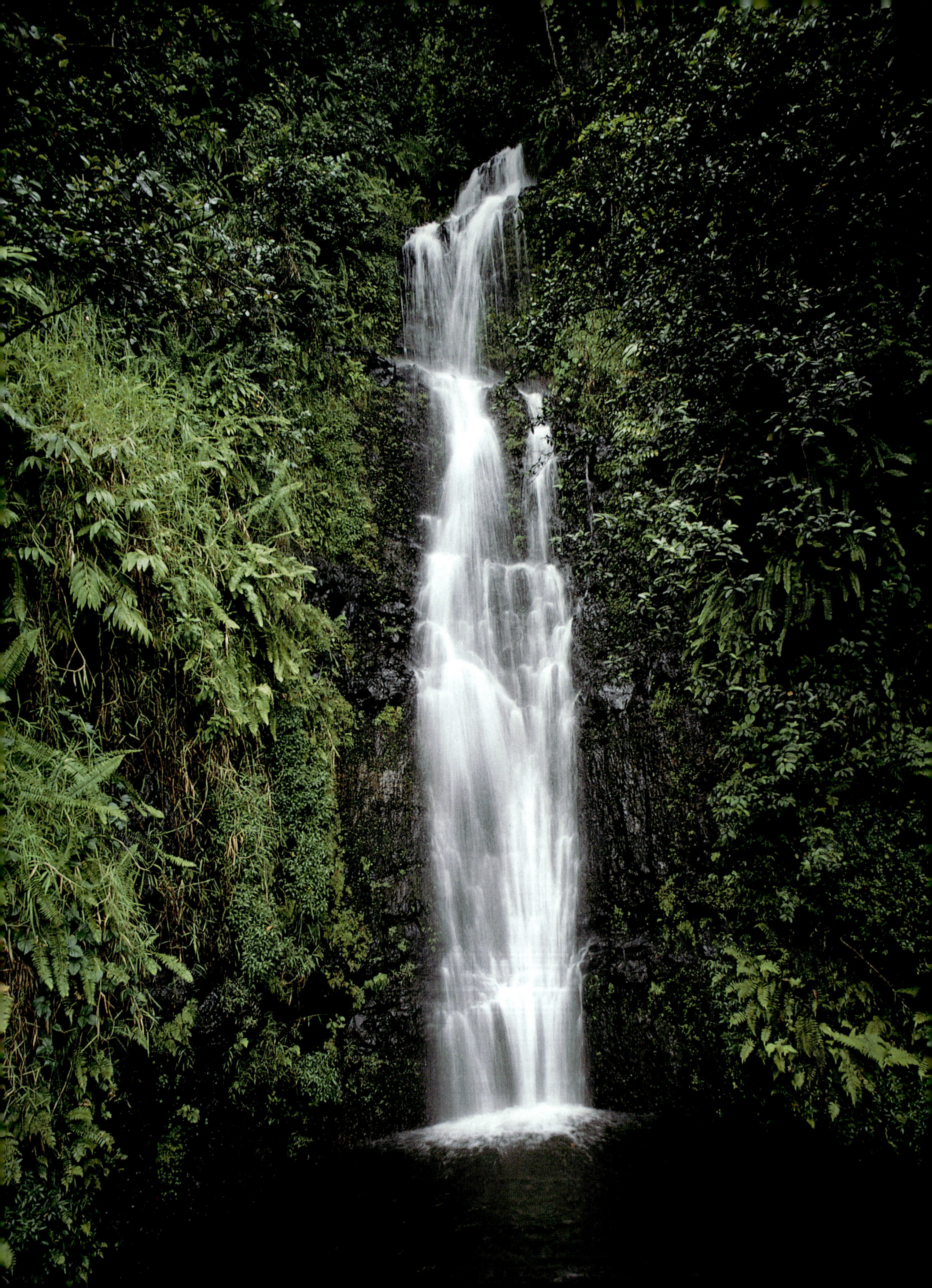

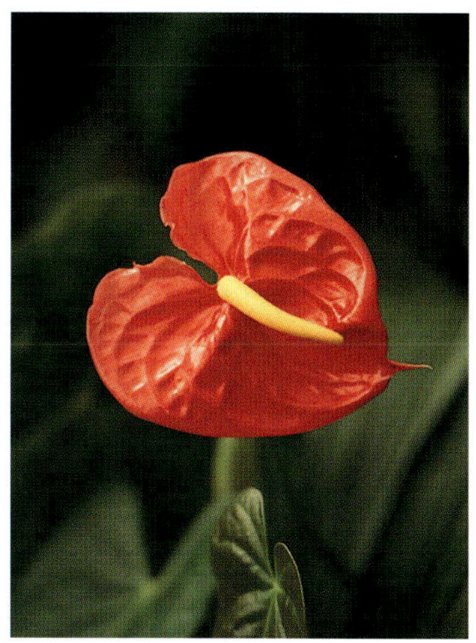

Maui

Thousands of centuries ago a volcano erupted deep within the Pacific Ocean. The flowing lava grew and grew, reaching the surface and then climbing high into the sky, creating Mauna Kahalawai. Soon, not far away, another eruption began growing even faster and further, reaching ten thousand feet above the water, to form Haleakala. The molten lava continued to flow between these giants, rising above the steaming ocean, connecting and giving birth to what would become a fertile isthmus and hundreds of lush valleys. All these centuries later tourists call it *Maui*, the "Valley Isle."

Ancient Hawaiian legends also say the half-god, half-man Maui used a magic fishhook to pull the Hawaiian Islands up from the sea. He then chose Haleakala as his home. It was an unlucky choice, because the days there were very short. This was because the sun was lazy, sleeping late and then racing across the sky. Maui snared the sun and held it hostage until it promised to go slower over his island. Now the sun rises very early and drifts slowly over *Haleakala*, meaning "House of the Sun" in Hawaiian.

Maui's natural beauty and the warmth of its seemingly endless sun make the legends come alive. World-class resorts, spectacular golf courses, nightlife, incredible water sports, and endless beaches also make Maui an irresistible destination. Hawaiians have called it the "Magic Isle," but many locals simply say *Maui no ka oi,* which means "Maui is the Best."

◁ *Numerous waterfalls line the 50-mile-long Hana highway.*
△ *Anthurium's wax-like blossoms last up to three weeks after cutting.*
▷ ▷ *A powerful winter wave crests along Maui's Maliko Bay.*

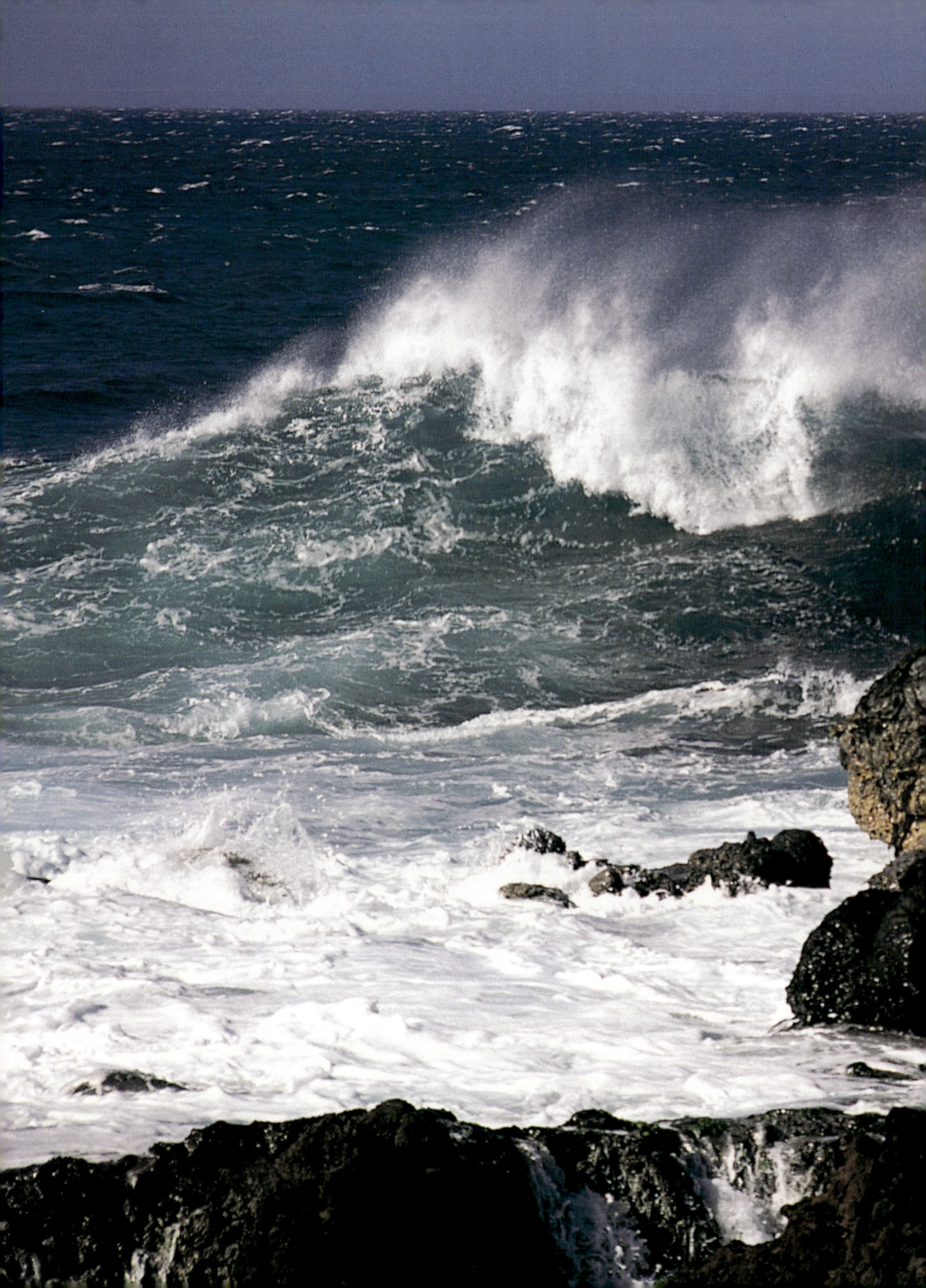

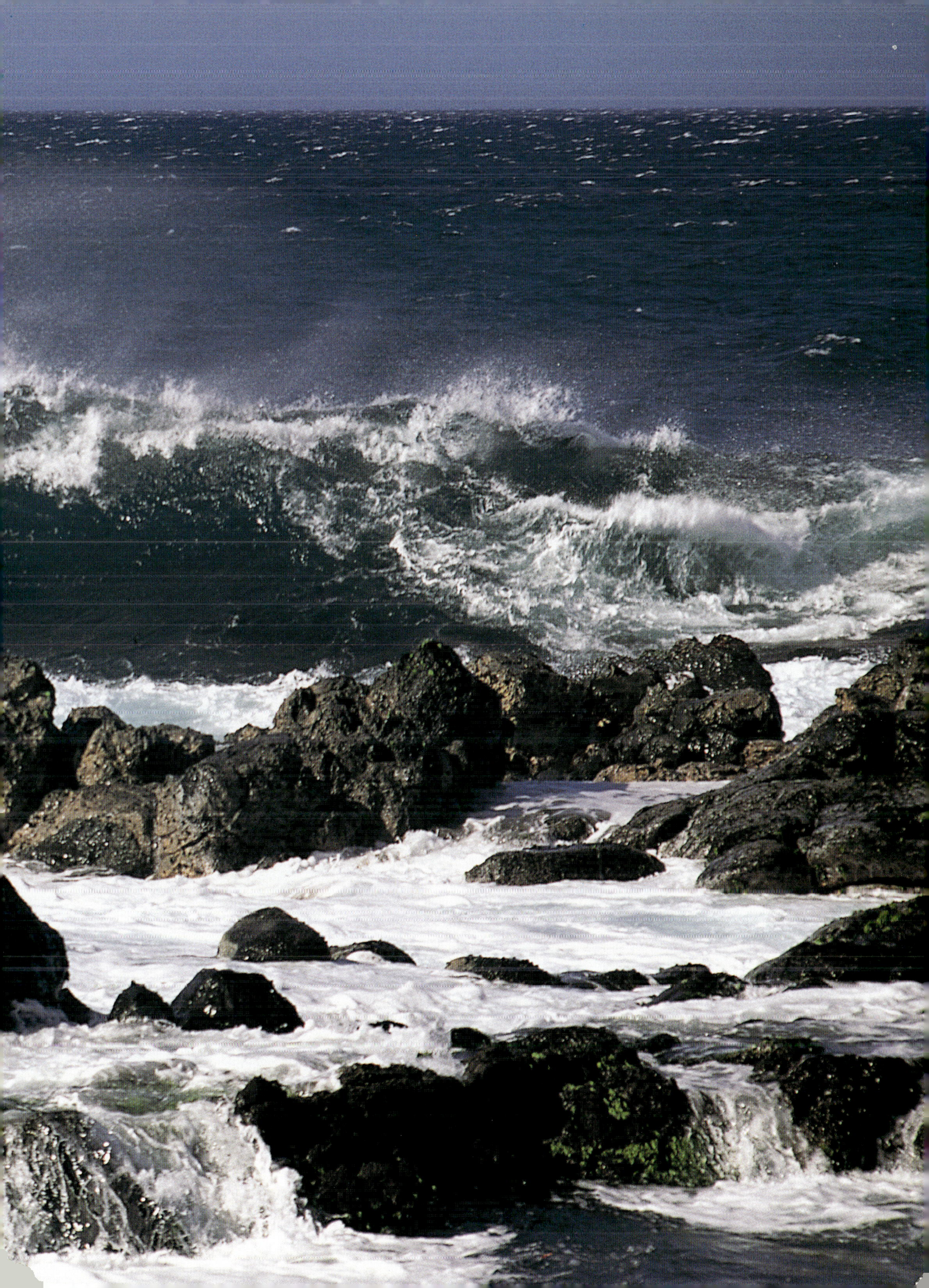

▽ Carp, edible freshwater fish originally from Europe and Asia, swim in a Maui pond. Popular throughout the islands, these colorful fish are treasured for their sense of tranquility. ▷ A ship sails at sunset between the islands. American Hawaiian Cruises offers several excursions through the Hawaiian archipelago. In addition, the sloop *Maile* departs from the Big Island, and the vintage steamship SS *Independence* sails from Honolulu's Aloha Tower.

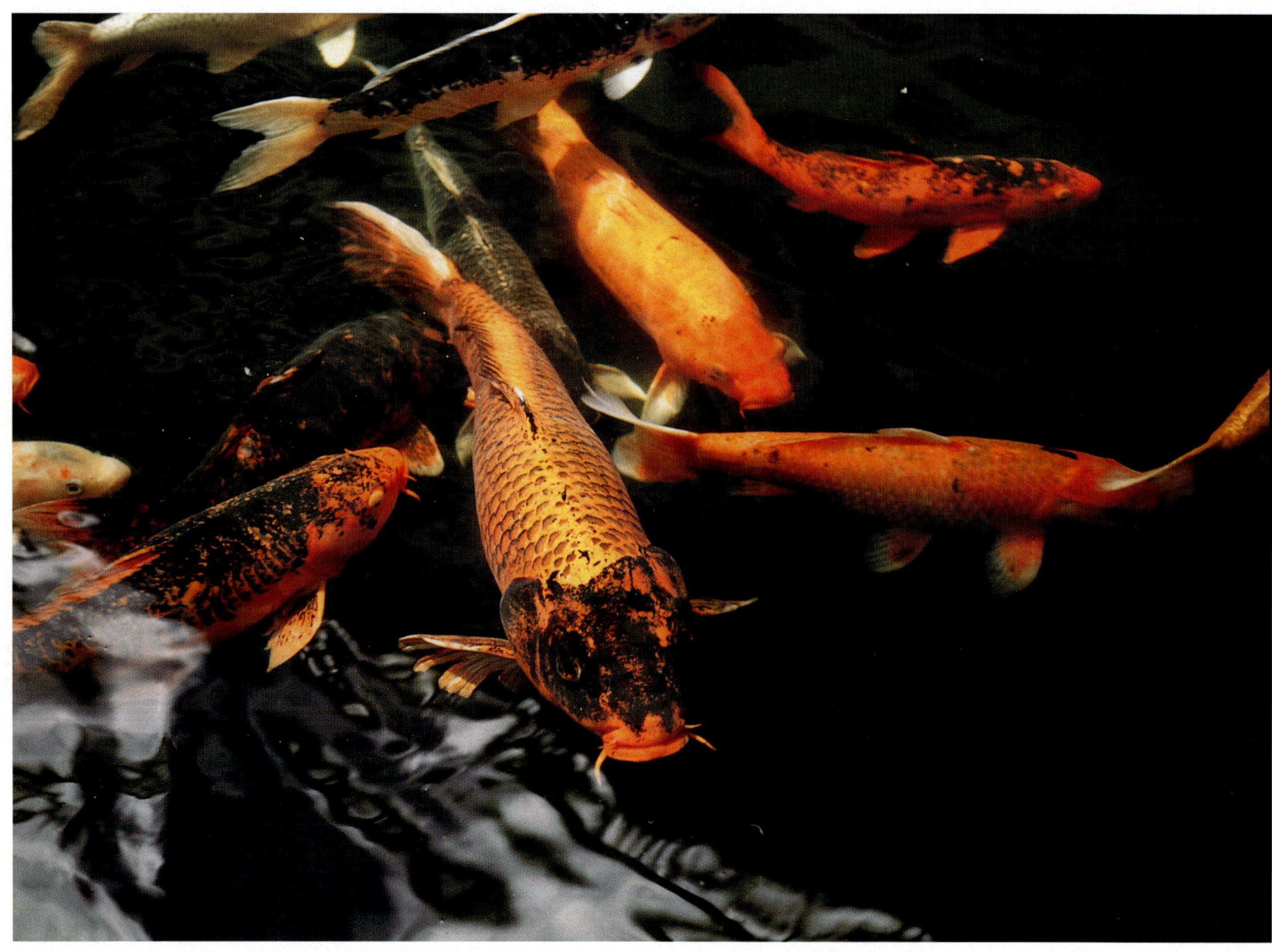

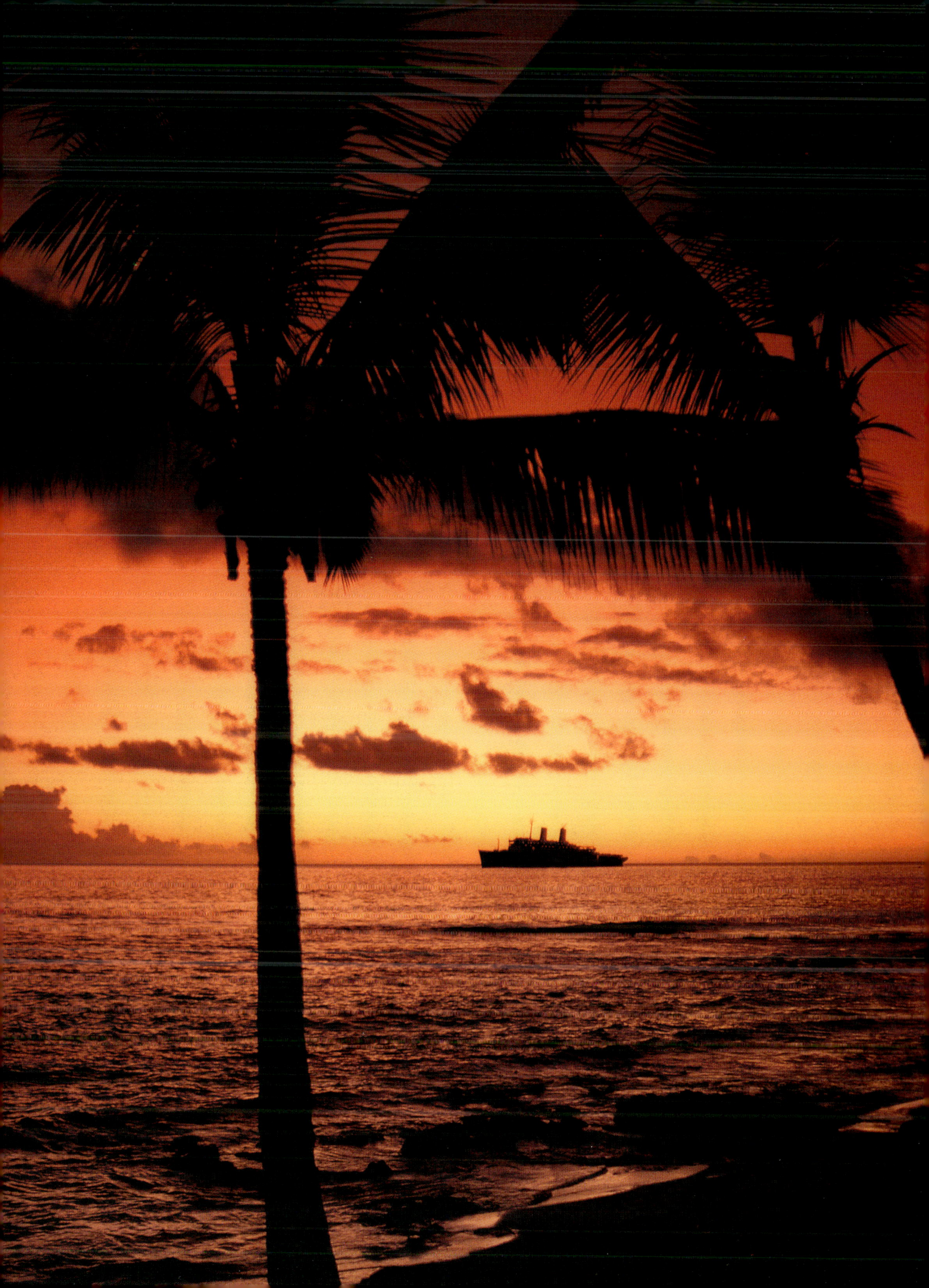

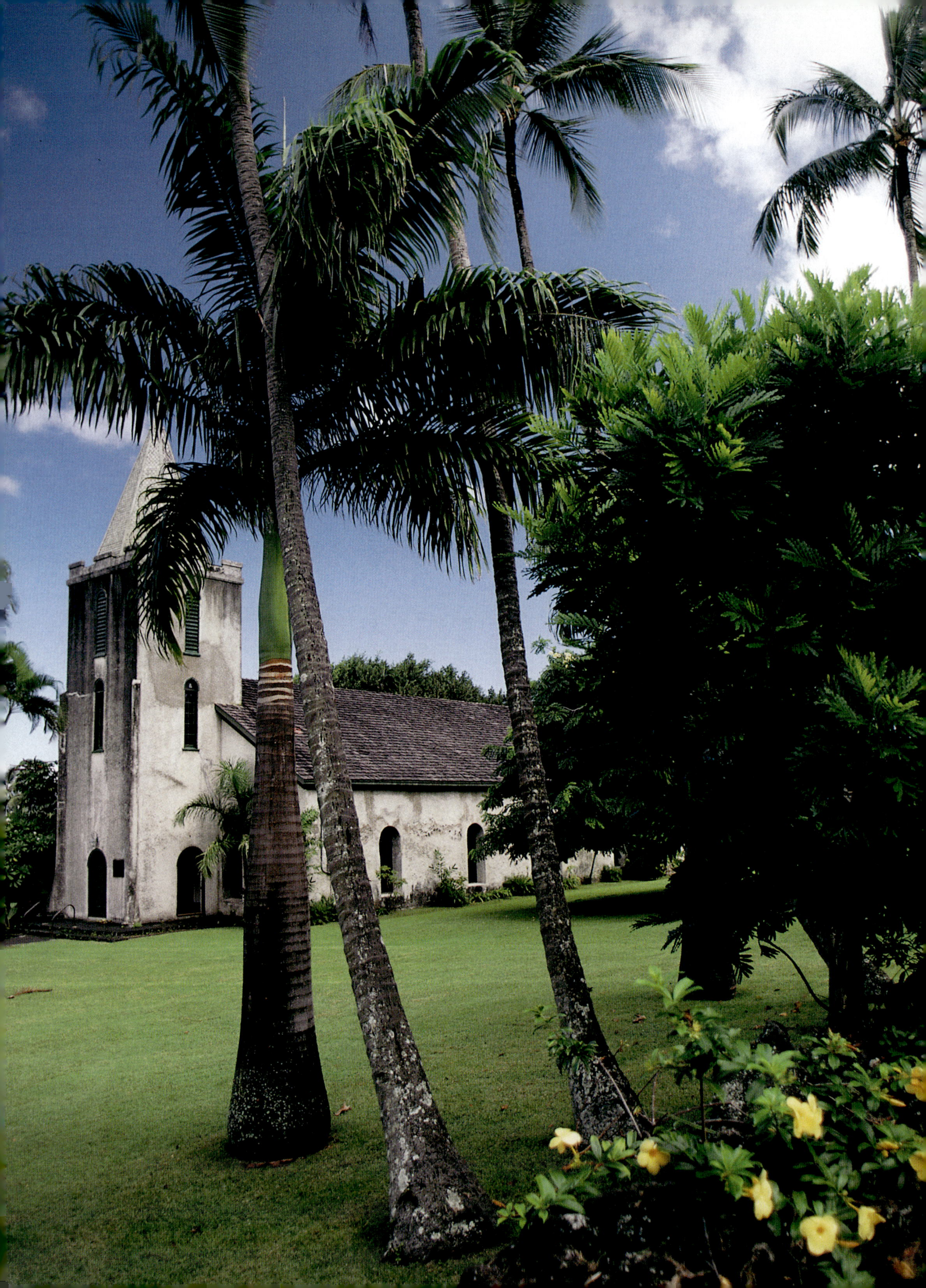

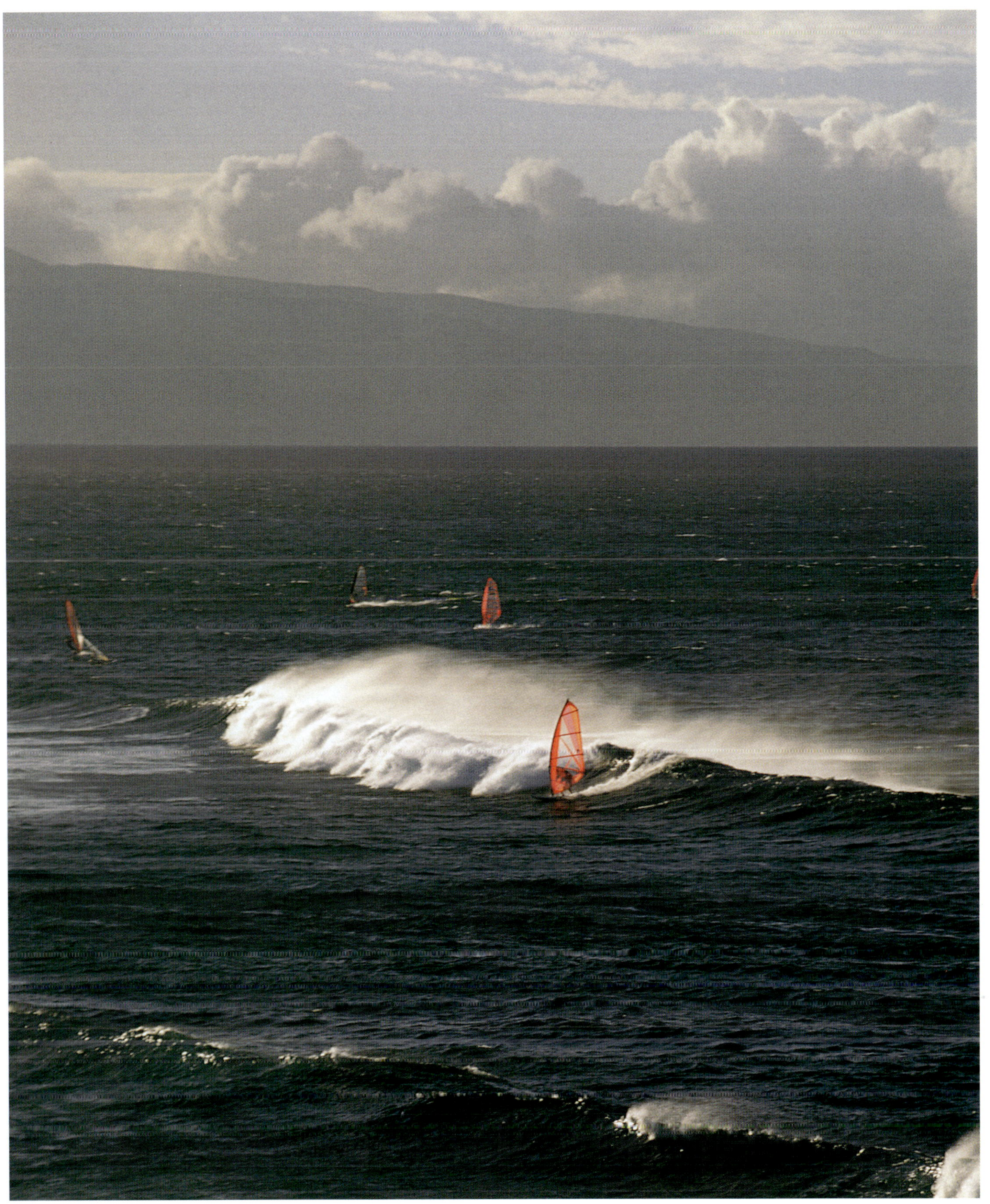

◁ The Wananalua Church, completed in 1857, sits quietly beside the road as one enters the village of Hana.
△ Windsurfers from around the world flock to Maui during the winter, headquartering in the nearby town of Paia. Clouds of floating sea mist, known as *ehukai,* are created by the brisk winds and large winter waves.

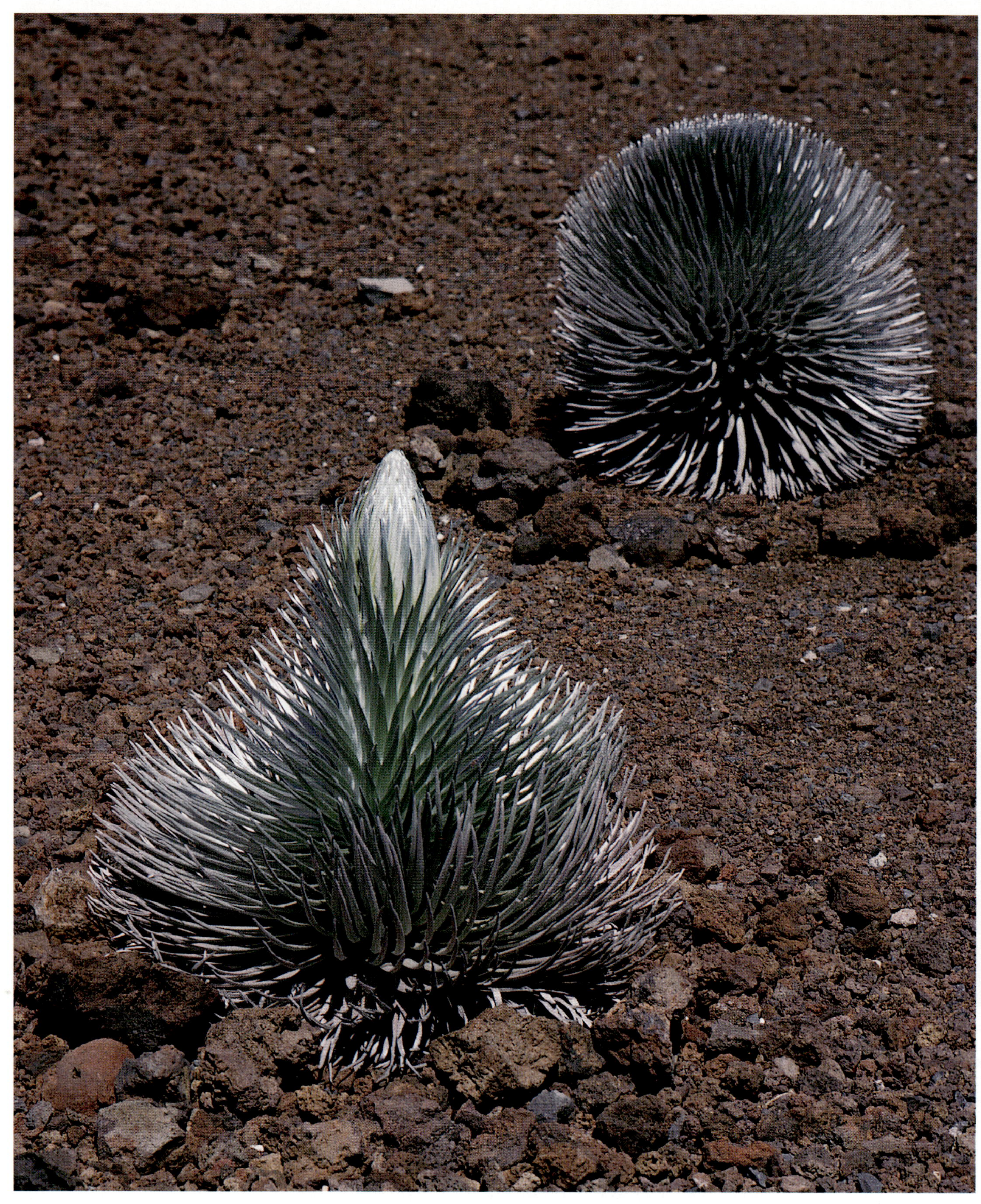

△ The endangered silversword grows only in Hawaii. It blooms once and then dies.
▷ Haleakala, or "House of the Sun," is classified as a dormant volcano.
Its last eruption is thought to have been in 1790.

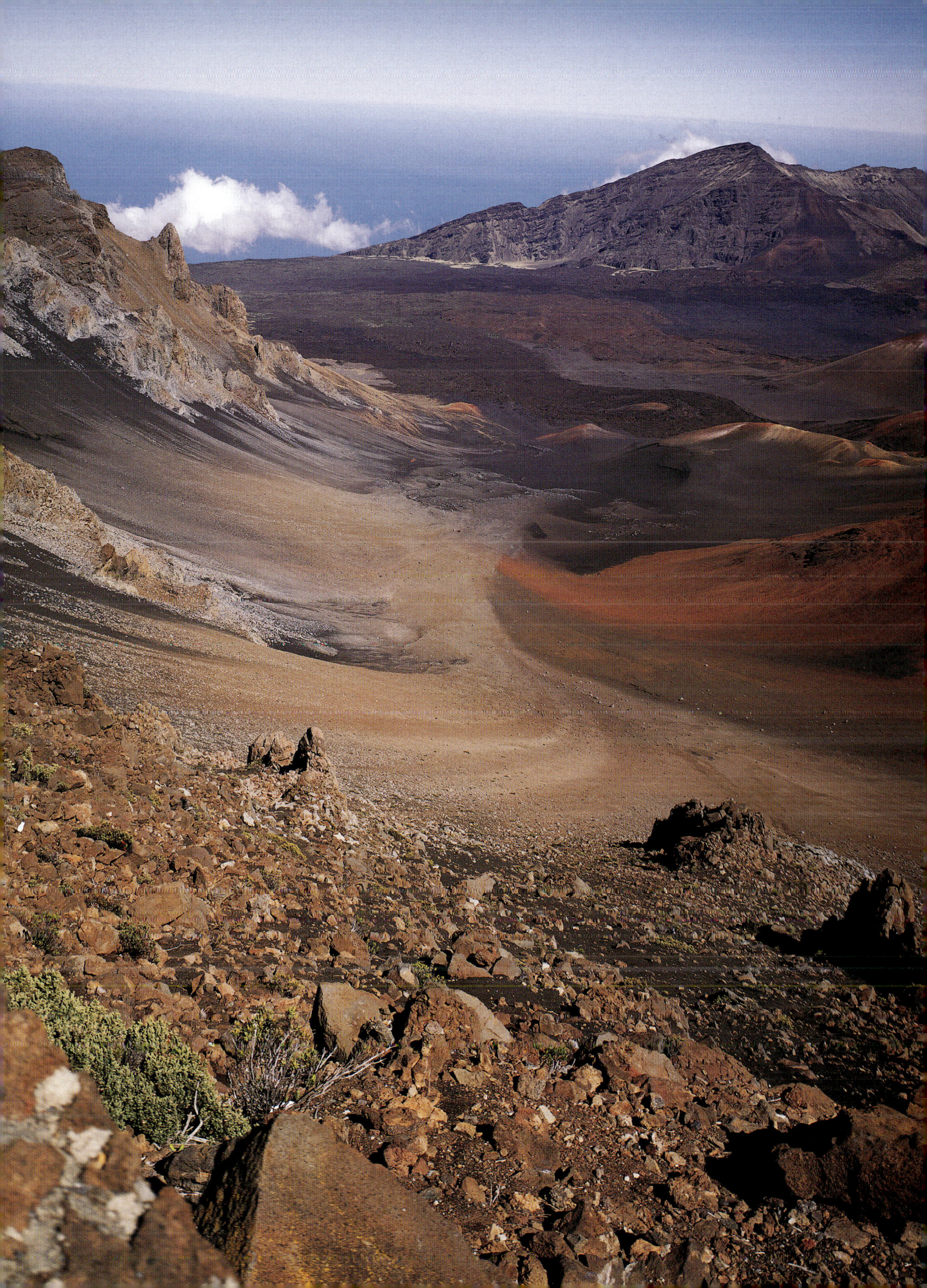

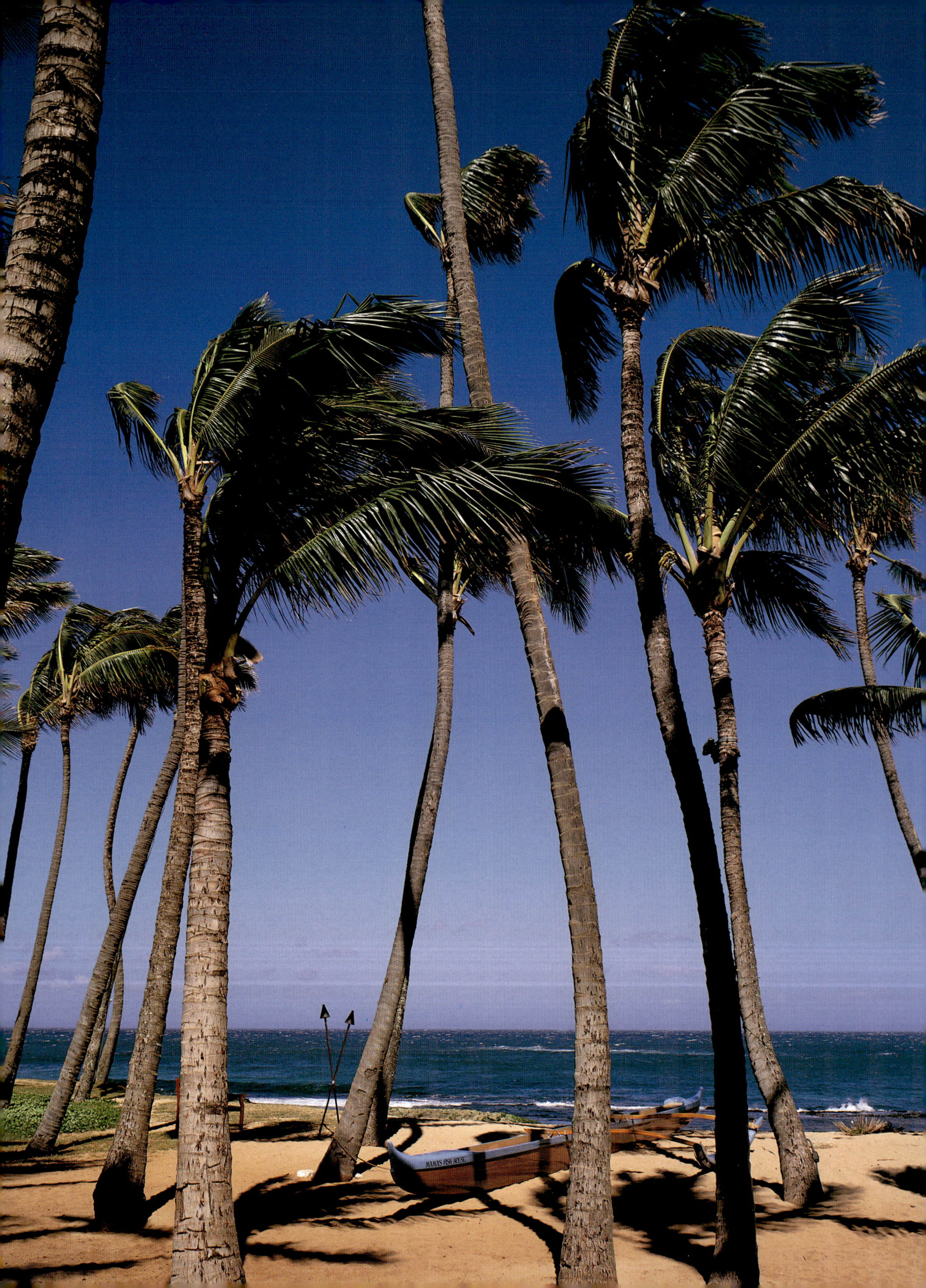
MAMA'S FISH HOUSE

◁ Just off the Hana highway at Kuau Cove, an outrigger canoe belonging to Mama's Fish House rests beneath tower palms.
▽ Although missionaries tried to stop all traditional Hawaiian customs, outrigger canoe racing and surfing not only survived but thrived. The Molokai to Oahu Canoe Race, an international paddling competition, takes place each year in October.

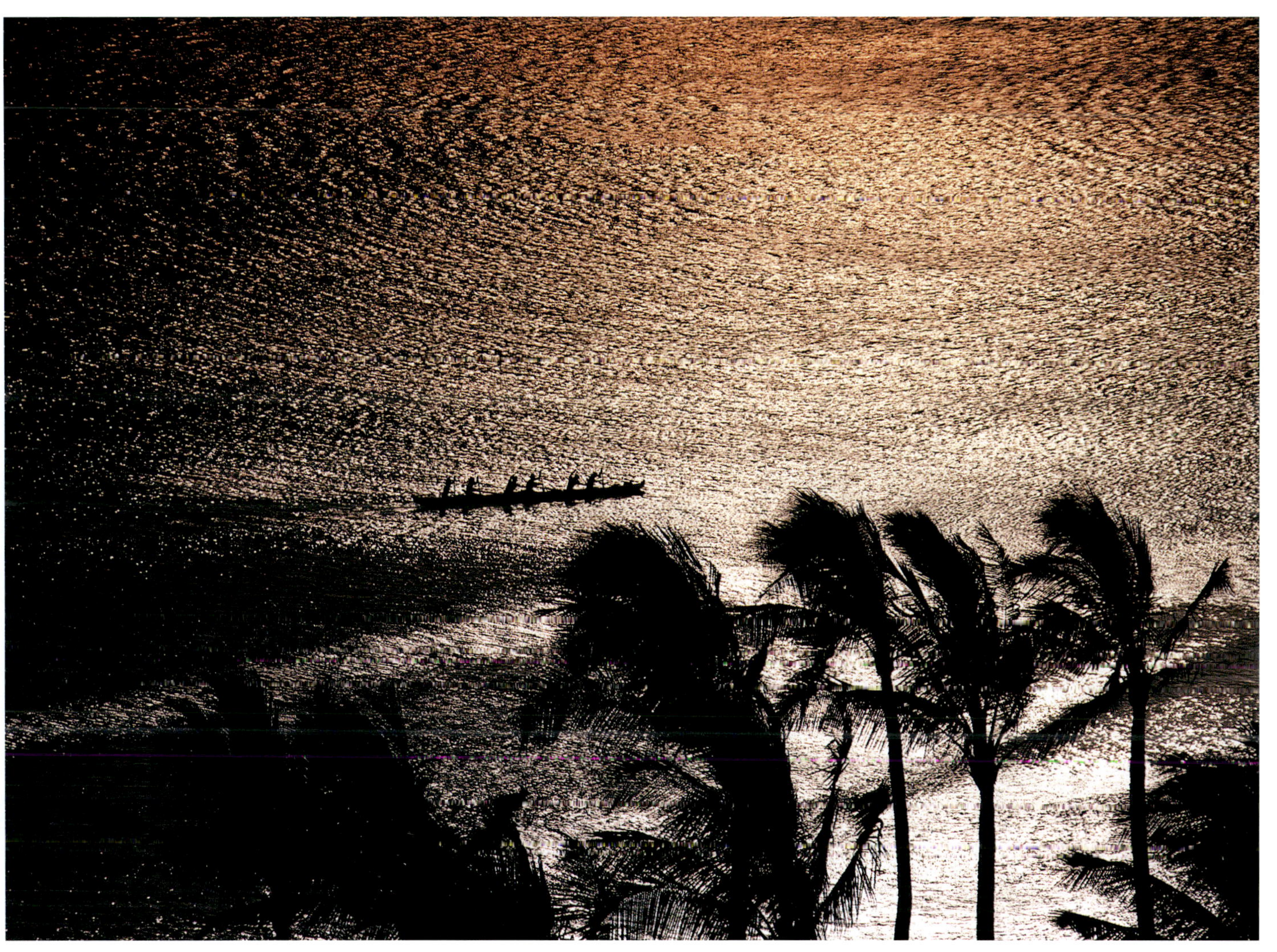

▽A humpback whale's tail, or fluke, rises from the water off the coast of Maui. An estimated 200 to 600 humpback whales visit the islands between November and the end of May each year.

▷ The flowering banana is a tree-like tropical plant that bears one bunch, then dies. Another plant then grows from new shoots around the base.

▷ ▷ Makena Beach is a great place to swim, surf, sunbathe, and enjoy the view of Lanai.

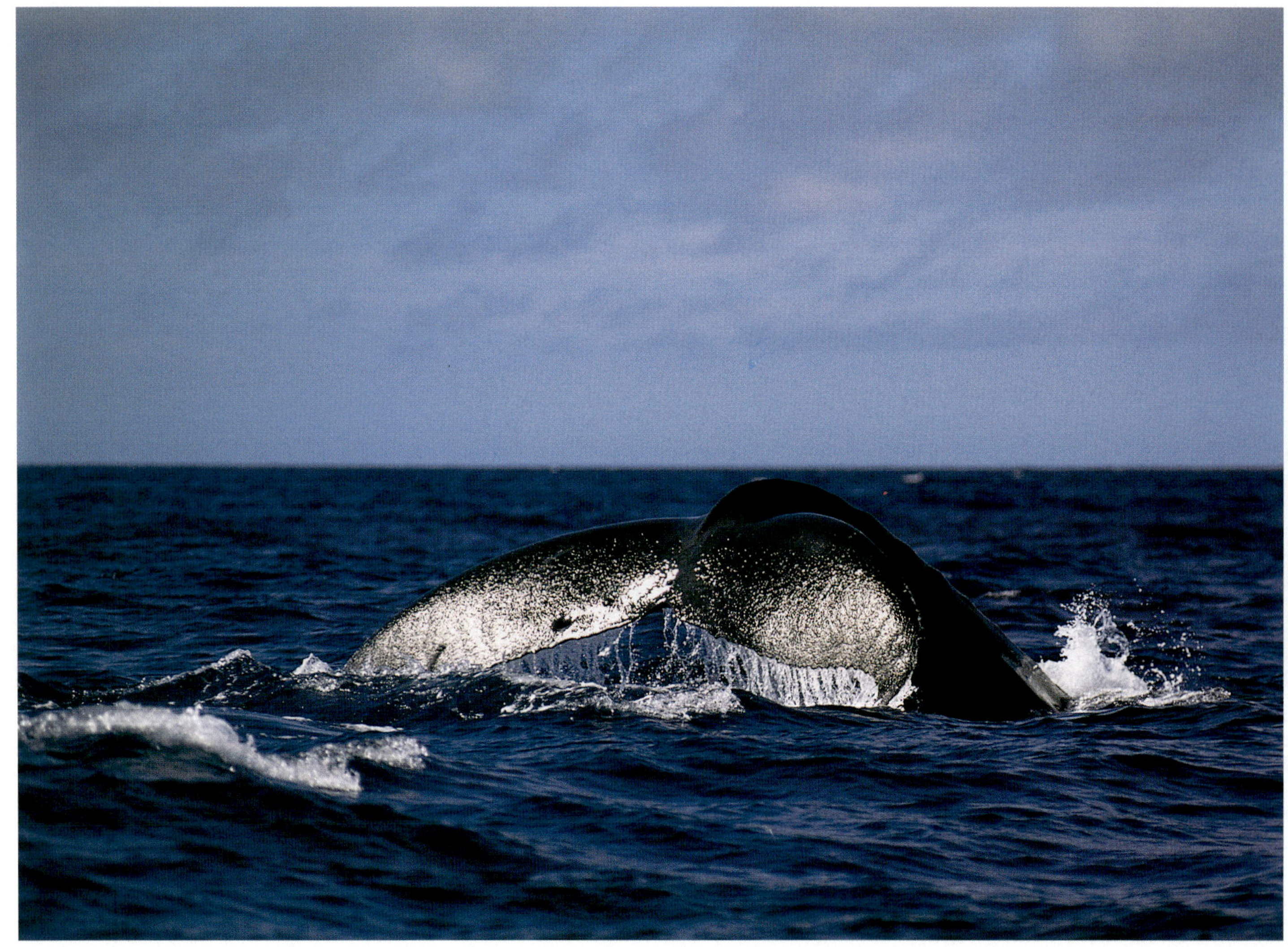

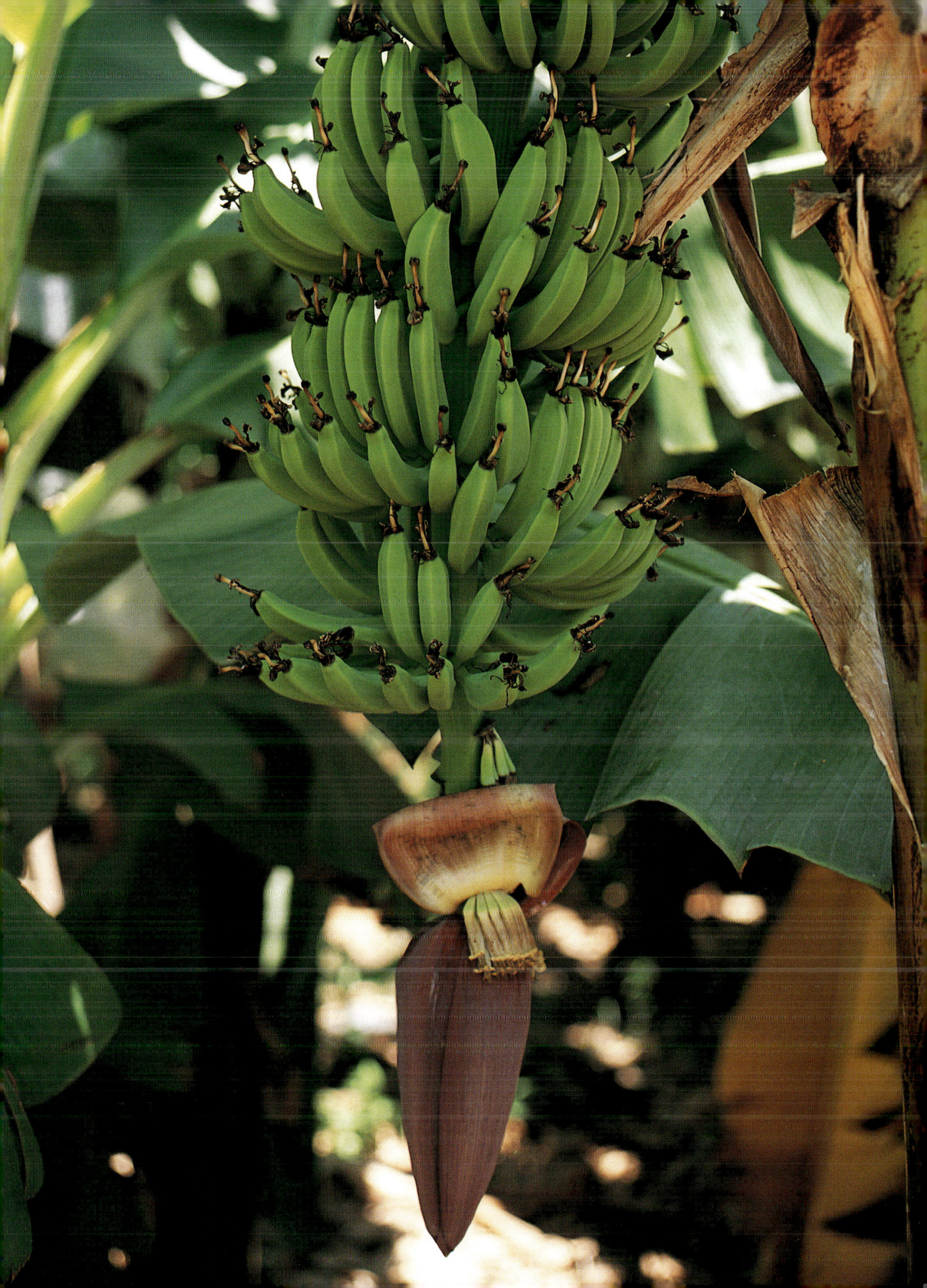

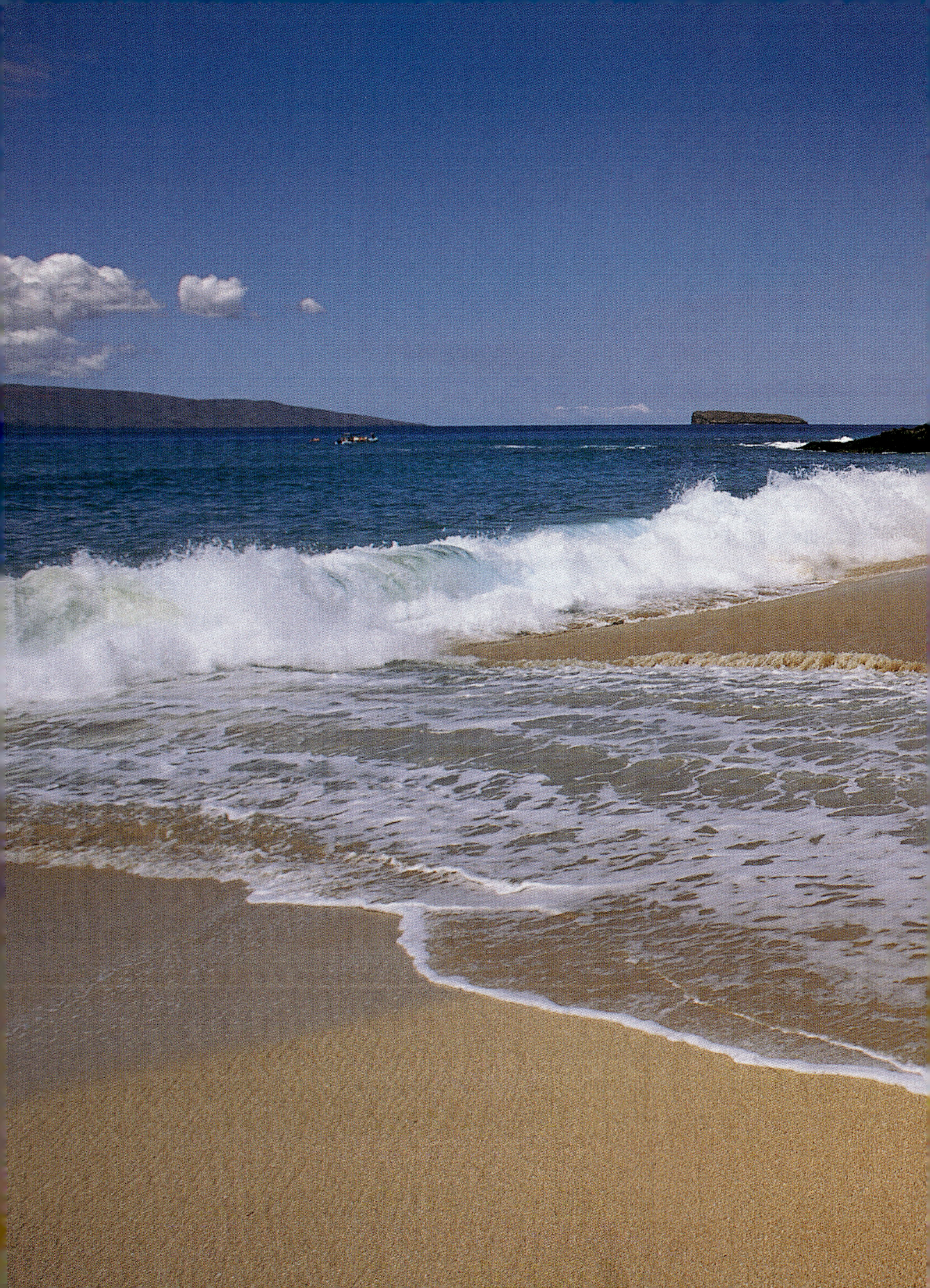

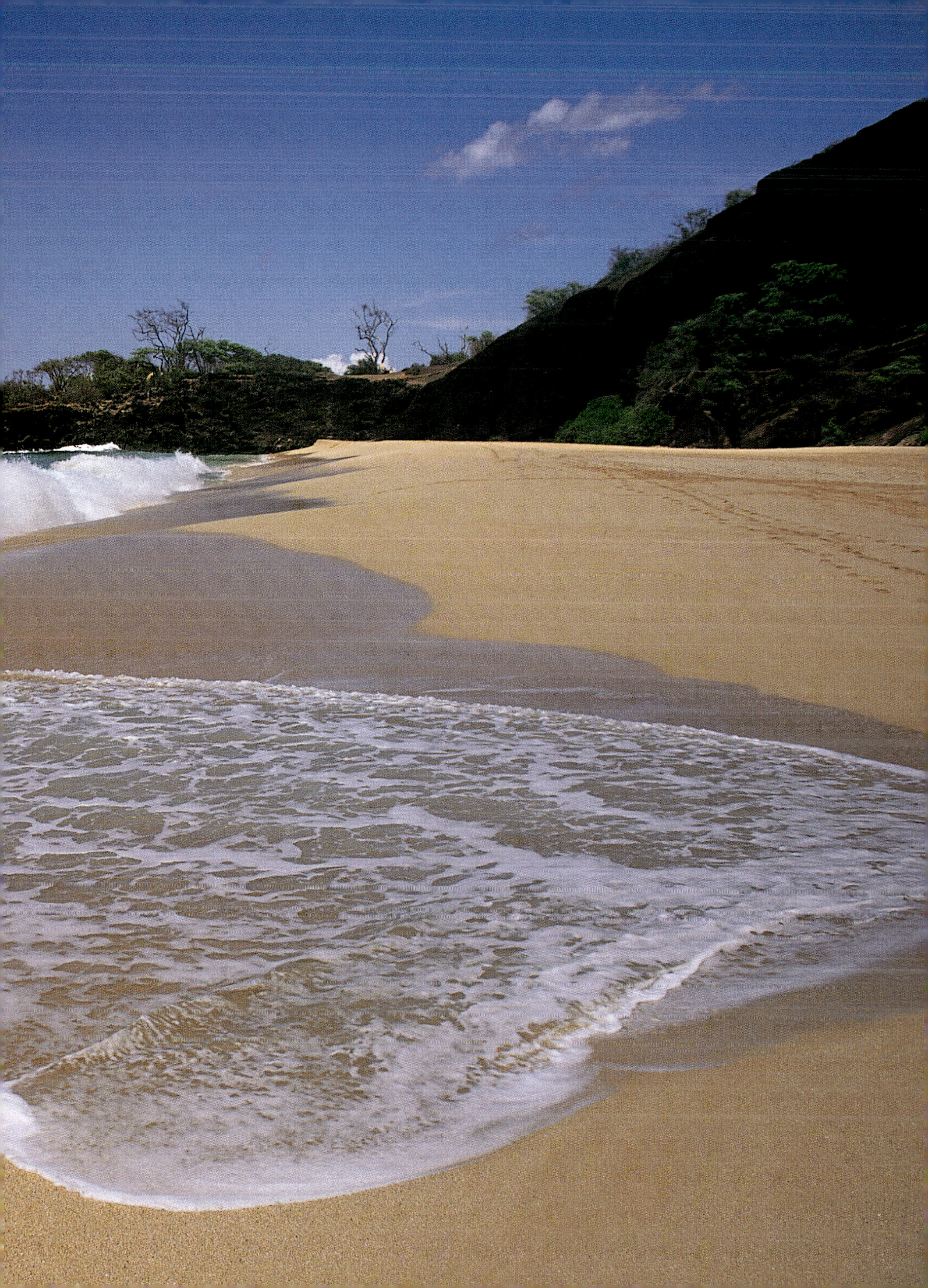

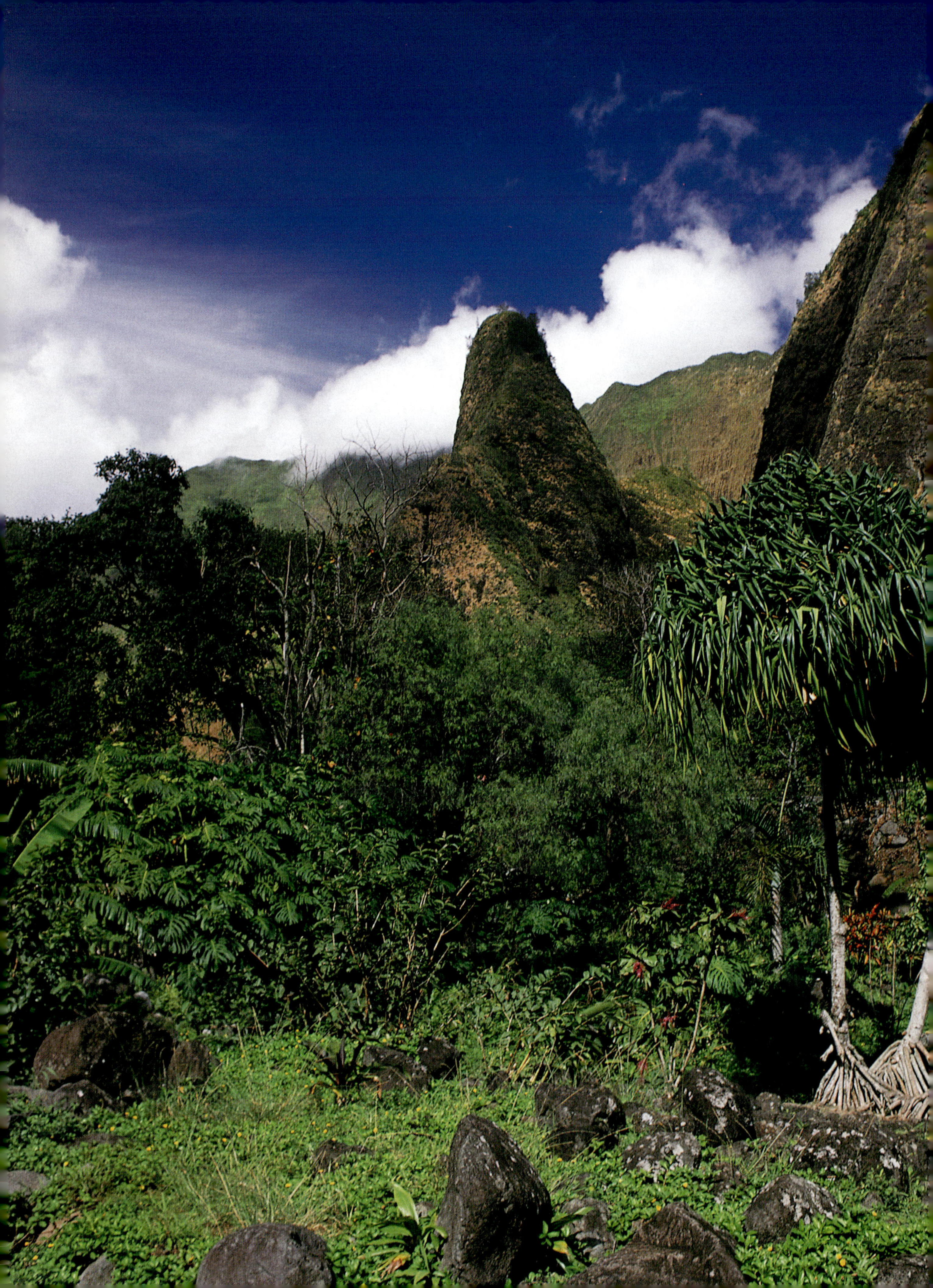

◁ Iao Needle rises 1200 feet from the valley floor. Situated in Iao Valley State Park in West Maui, the Needle is the centerpiece of a volcanic crater. The volcano that formed it created this part of the island. ▽ Perched along the water's edge, buildings such as these are part of the attraction of West Maui's Lahaina. The area was designated a National Historic Landmark in 1962.

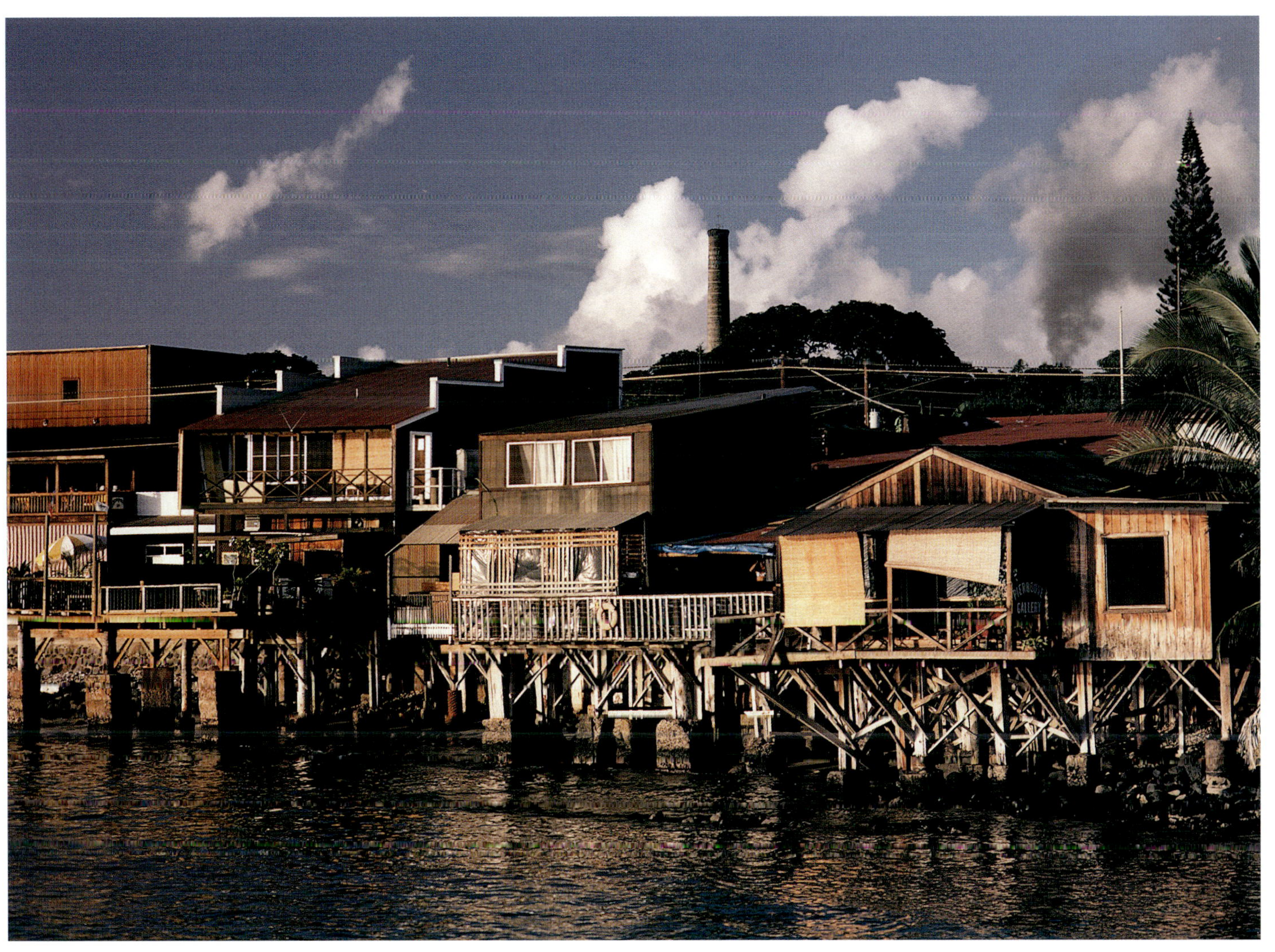

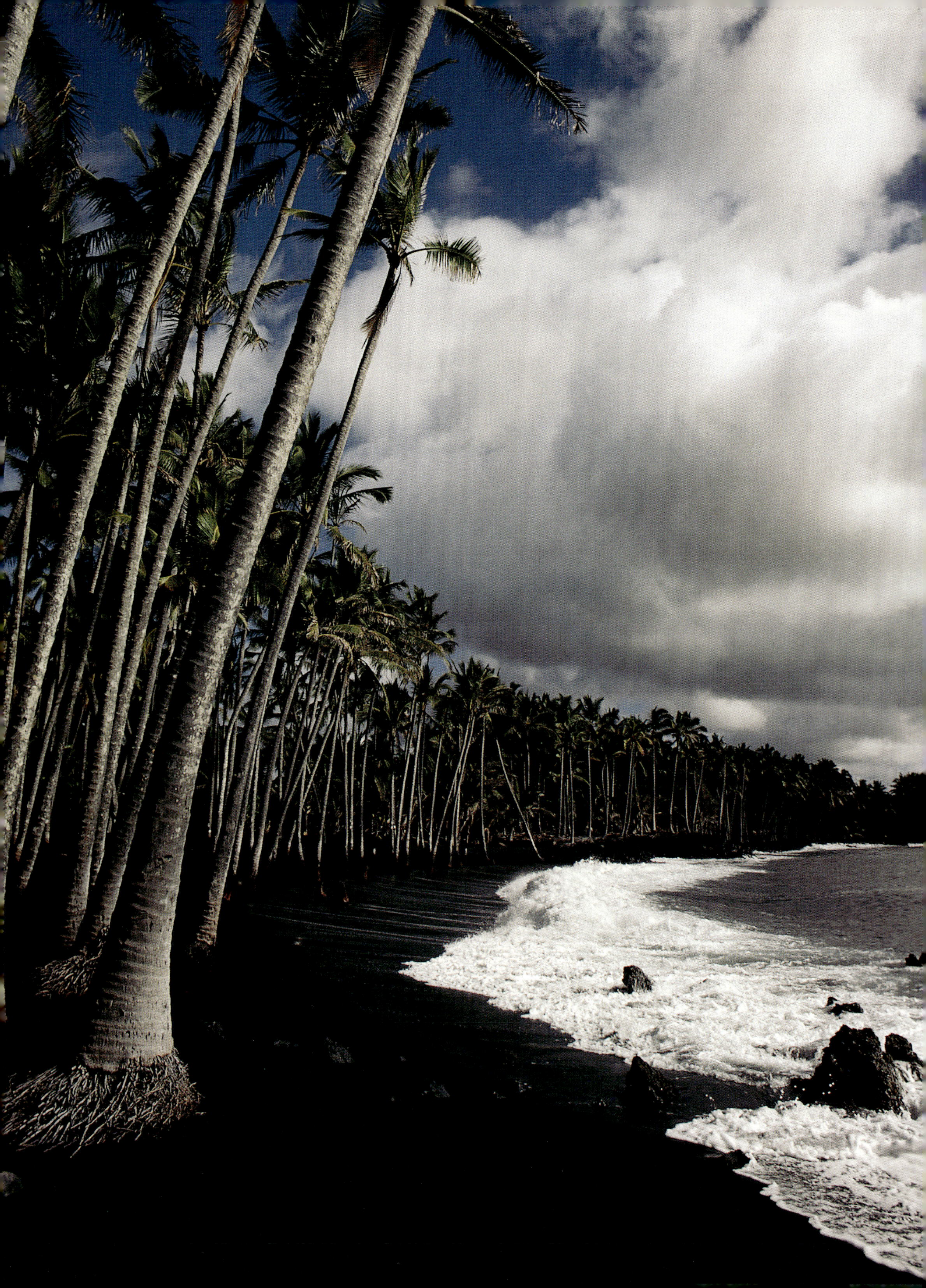

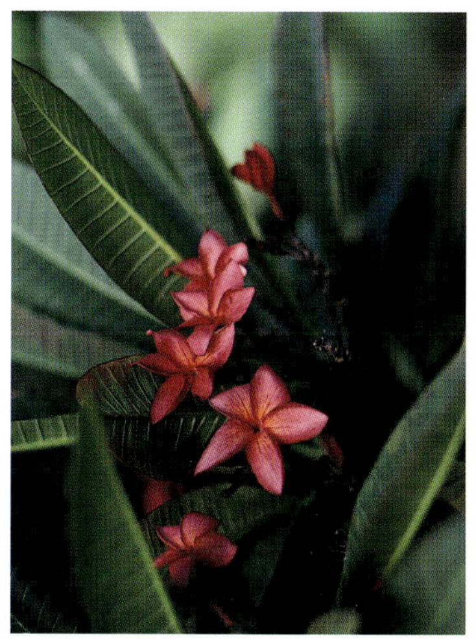

Big Island

When the first Polynesians landed on a huge island of steaming volcanoes, they called it *Hawai'ia,* "The Burning Hawaii." Today the Island of Hawaii is simply called the "Big Island." At twice the size of all other Hawaiian islands put together, it is the largest island in the Pacific Ocean . . . and it is growing every day.

The vast diversity within the Big Island's shores has prompted people to call it such things as the "Orchid Isle," the "Volcano Island," the "*Paniolo* (or 'cowboy') Island," and the "Sunset Island." All of these names describe parts of this amazing place, yet watching the earth being formed before your eyes, you find that no label is sufficient.

The Big Island has played an important role in the history of the Hawaiian Islands. In addition to being the first island discovered by Polynesians, it was the birthplace of Kamehameha, Hawaii's greatest king. Here he began the quest to unite all Hawaiians.

While all of the Hawaiian islands enjoy an extraordinary history of human evolution and development, most of them are complete, geologically speaking. The Big Island is just getting started. With each passing day, the island's physical wonders grow and change, as volcanic action takes place. Many ponder what manner of beauty and wonders will exist in fifteen or twenty million years, when the Big Island reaches the current age of its lush siblings.

◁ *On the Big Island, Kilauea Volcano sends lava flows into the sea, creating black-sand beaches such as this one at Kalapana.*
△ *Plumeria—white, pink, crimson, or yellow—blooms year-round.*

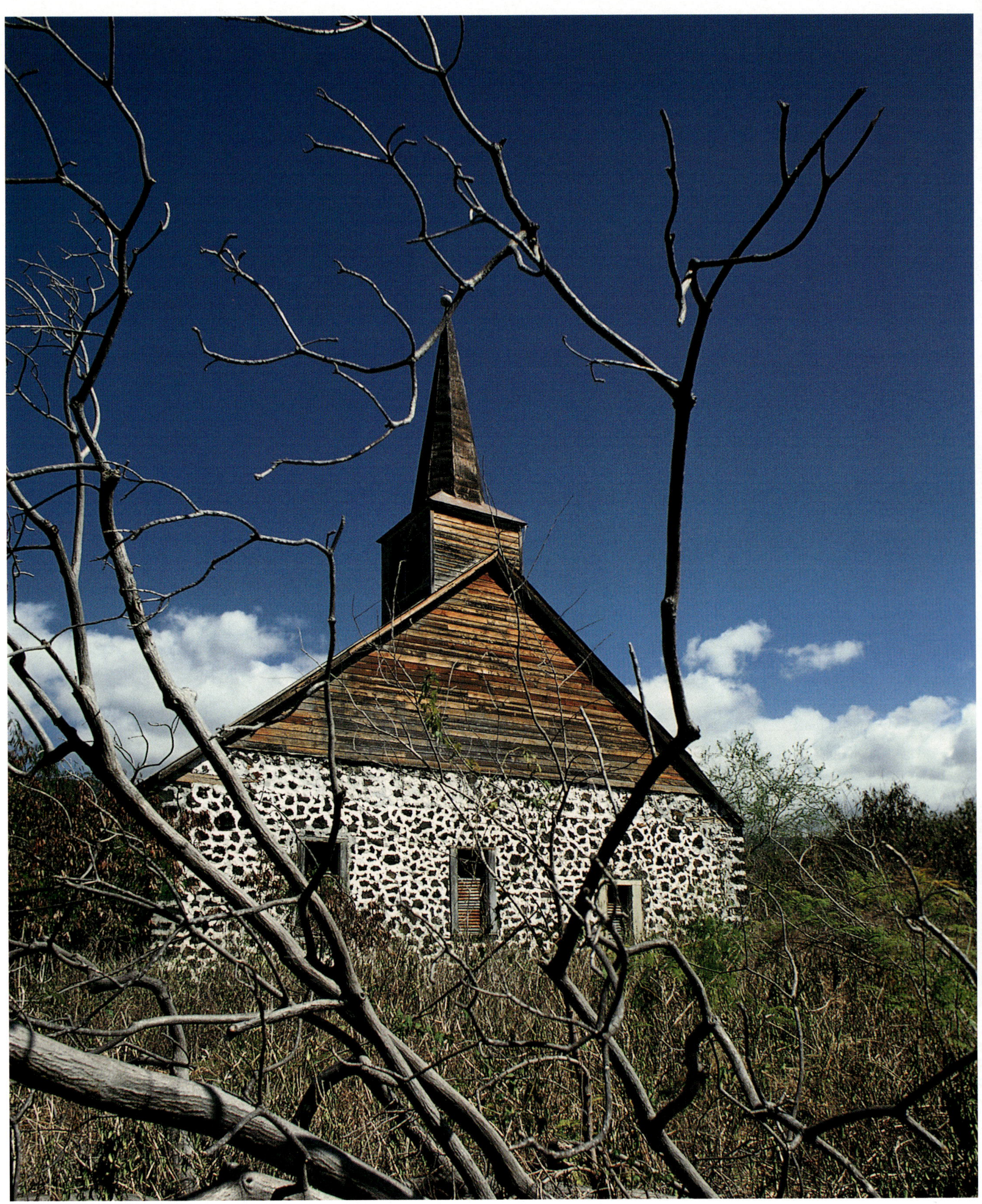

△ The Kahikolua Church, situated at Keei on the hill overlooking Kealakekua Bay, was completed in 1841.
▷ *Paniolos*, or "cowboys," work cattle on the Parker Ranch, one of the largest privately owned ranches in the United States.
▷ ▷ Snorkeling is popular in the clear emerald and blue waters of Kealakekua Bay, a state marine preserve.

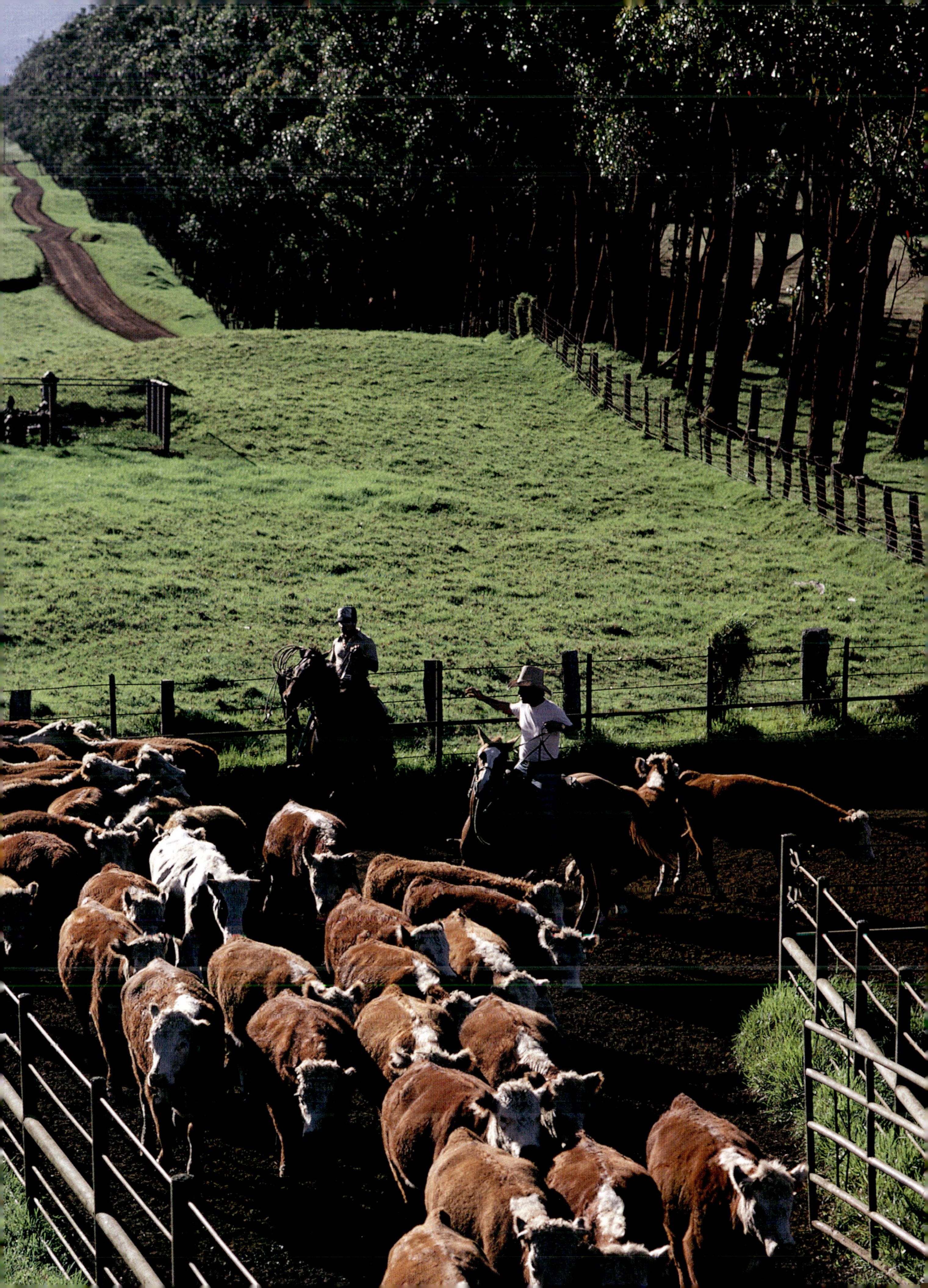

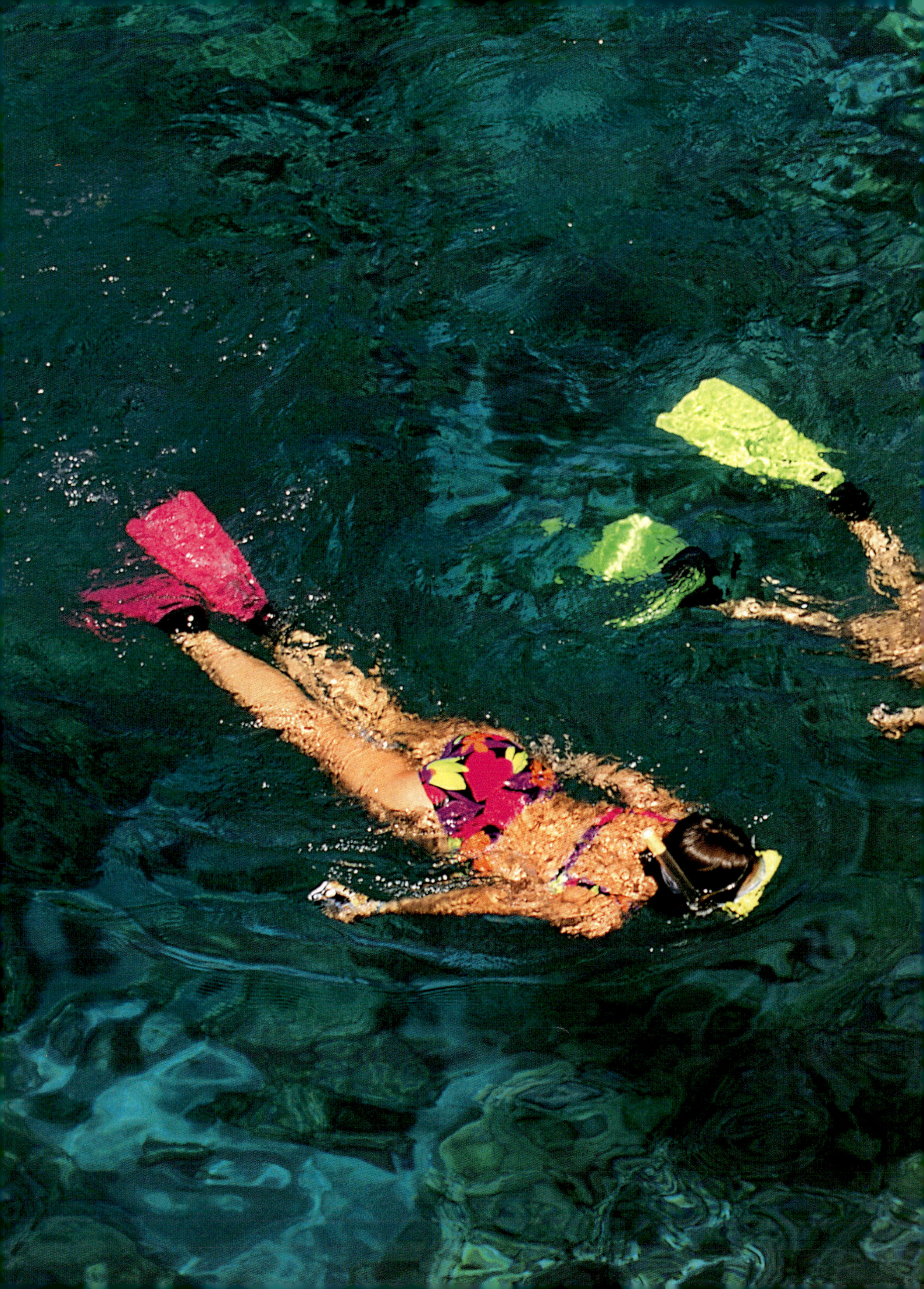

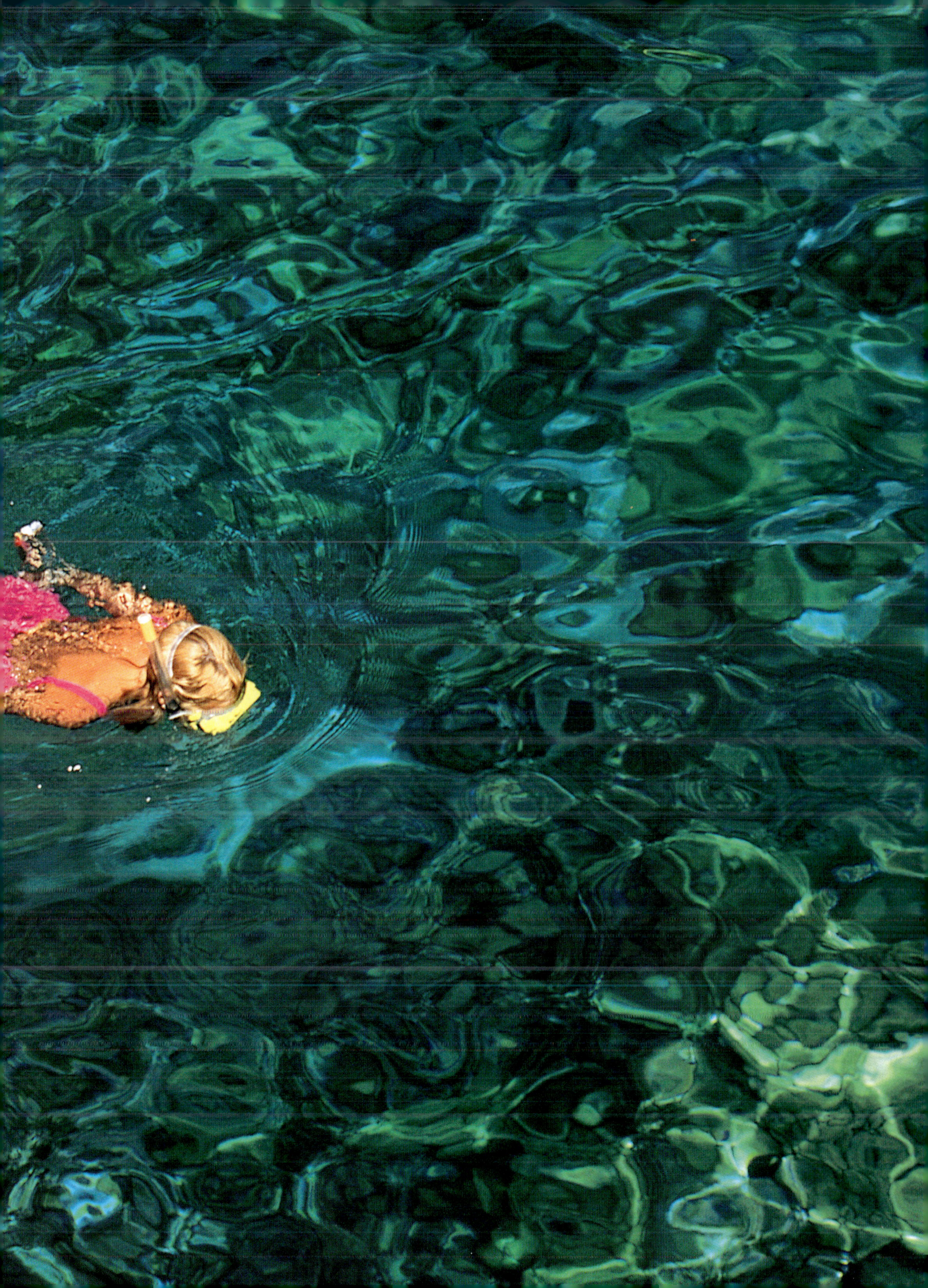

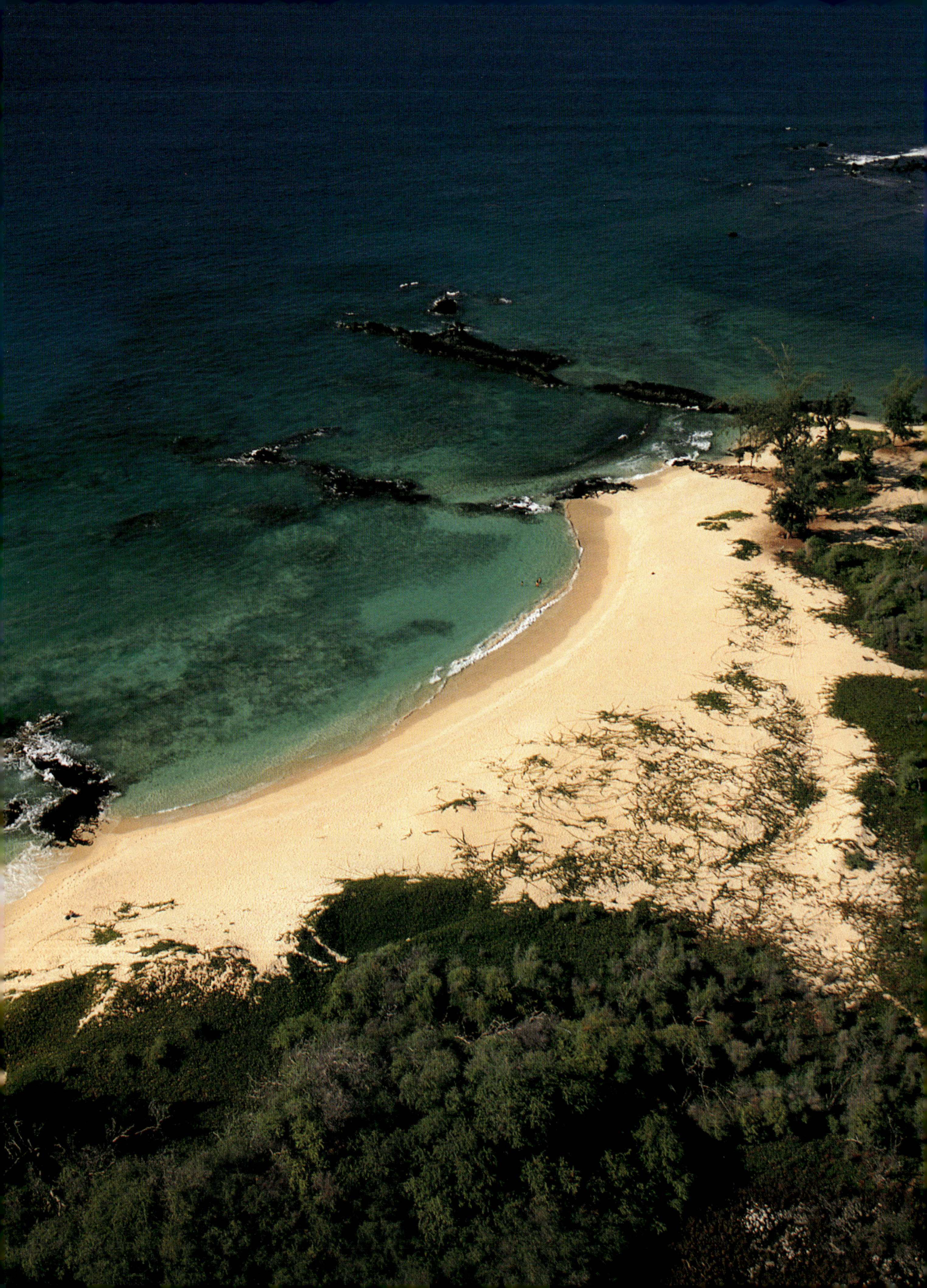

◁ Kea Beach, located along the Kohala coastline, is reached either by water or by four-wheel-drive vehicles crossing the lava flow. This golden-sand stretch of beach is a secluded getaway for local residents.
▽ A fisherman casts his net into the waters off Hapuna Beach State Park. The largest beach on the Big Island, its golden sands stretch for more than half a mile. The waters here are gentle in summer, but winter brings waves too strong for swimming.

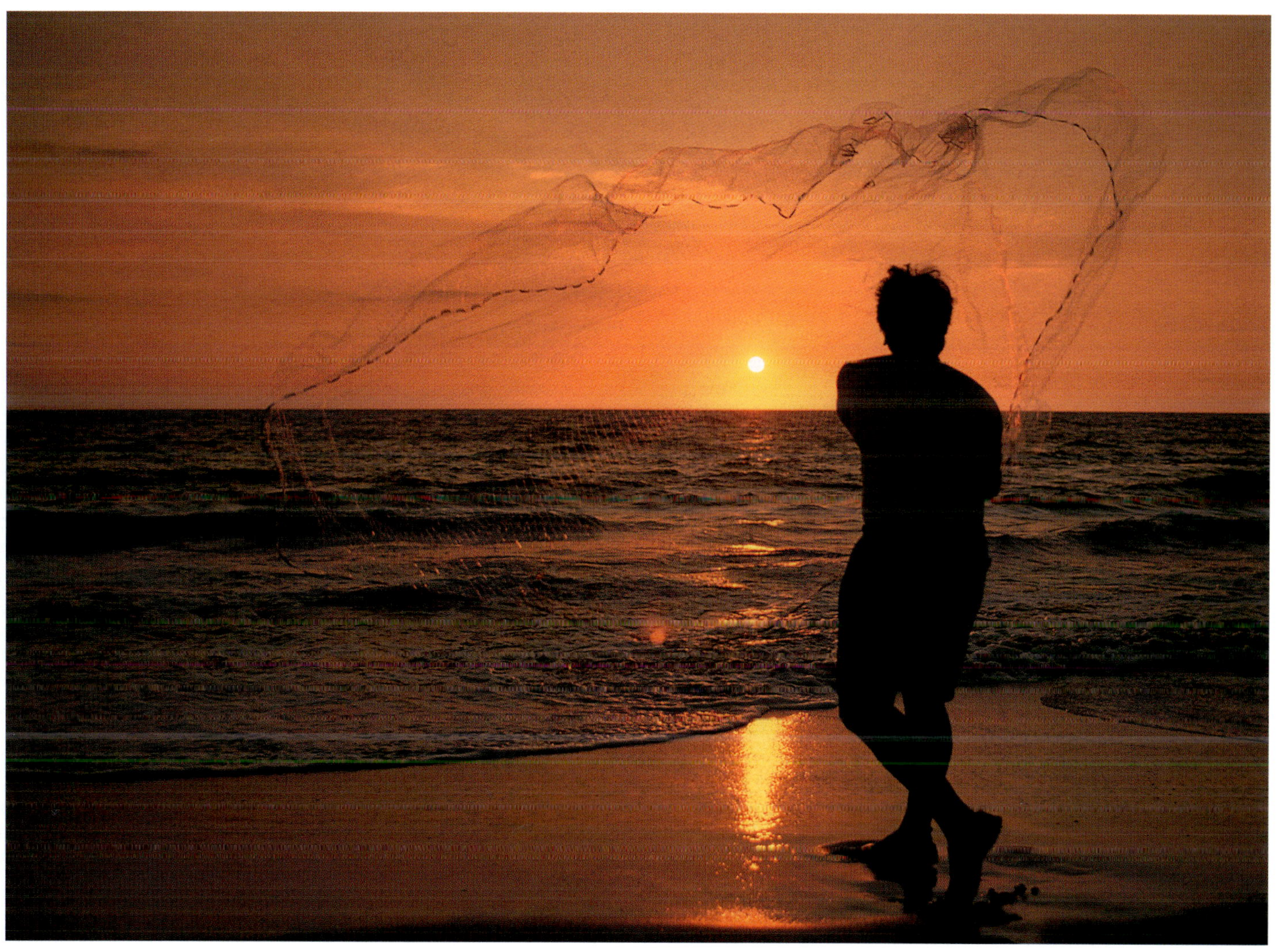

▽ Kehena Black Sand Beach is not far down the coast from Hilo, the Big Island's largest city. Access to the beach requires a steep hike down a rocky path from a neighborhood street, making its secluded sands difficult to find. ▷ Kii, glowering wooden images of old Hawaii, guard the temple and grounds of *Puuhonua o Honaunau,* the "Place of Refuge." Centuries ago, defeated warriors and breakers of the *kapu,* the strict system of social codes, could escape the wrath of local chiefs, or *alii,* if they could make it to a sacred "place of refuge." After absolution, the offender could return to society.

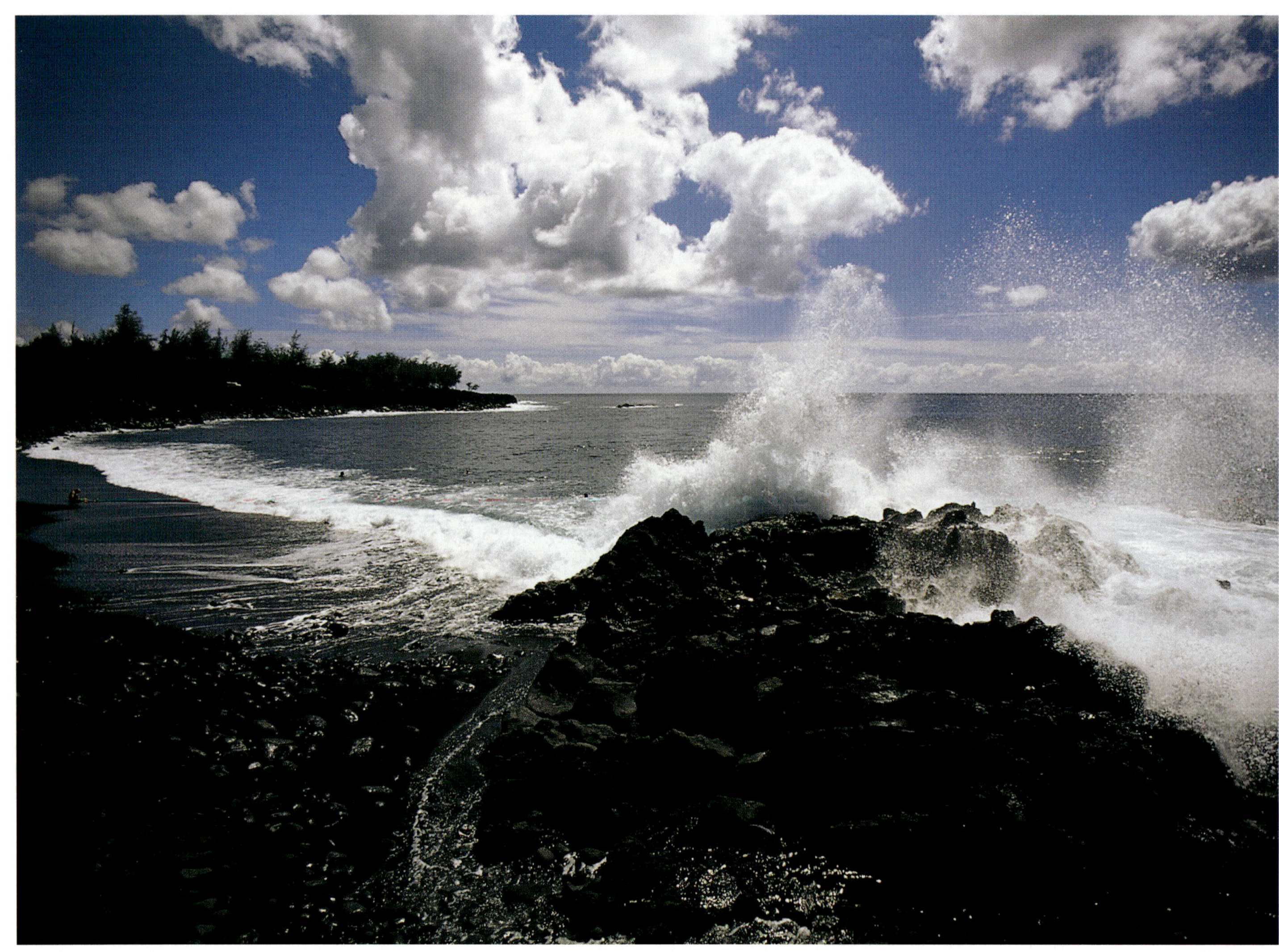

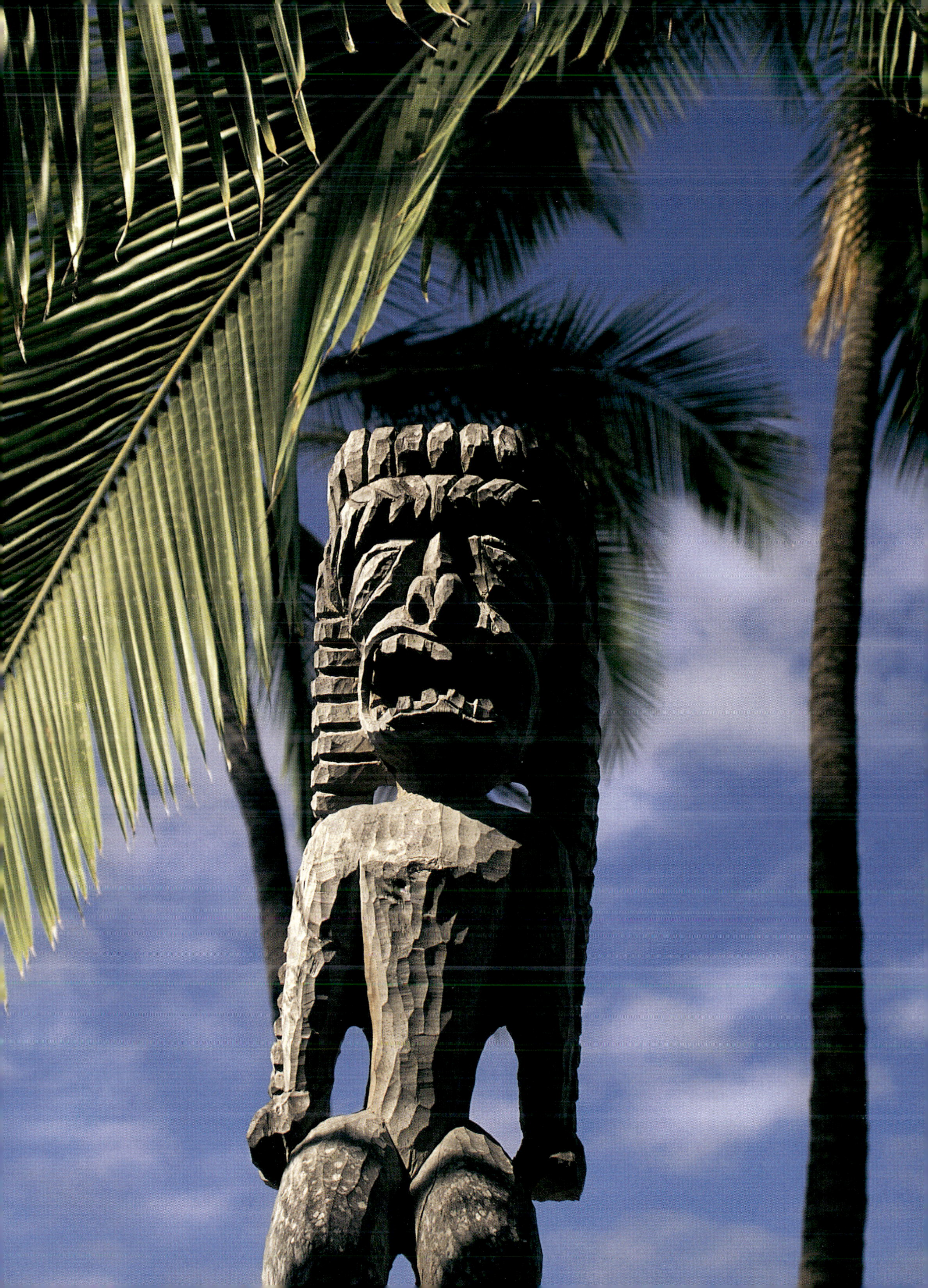

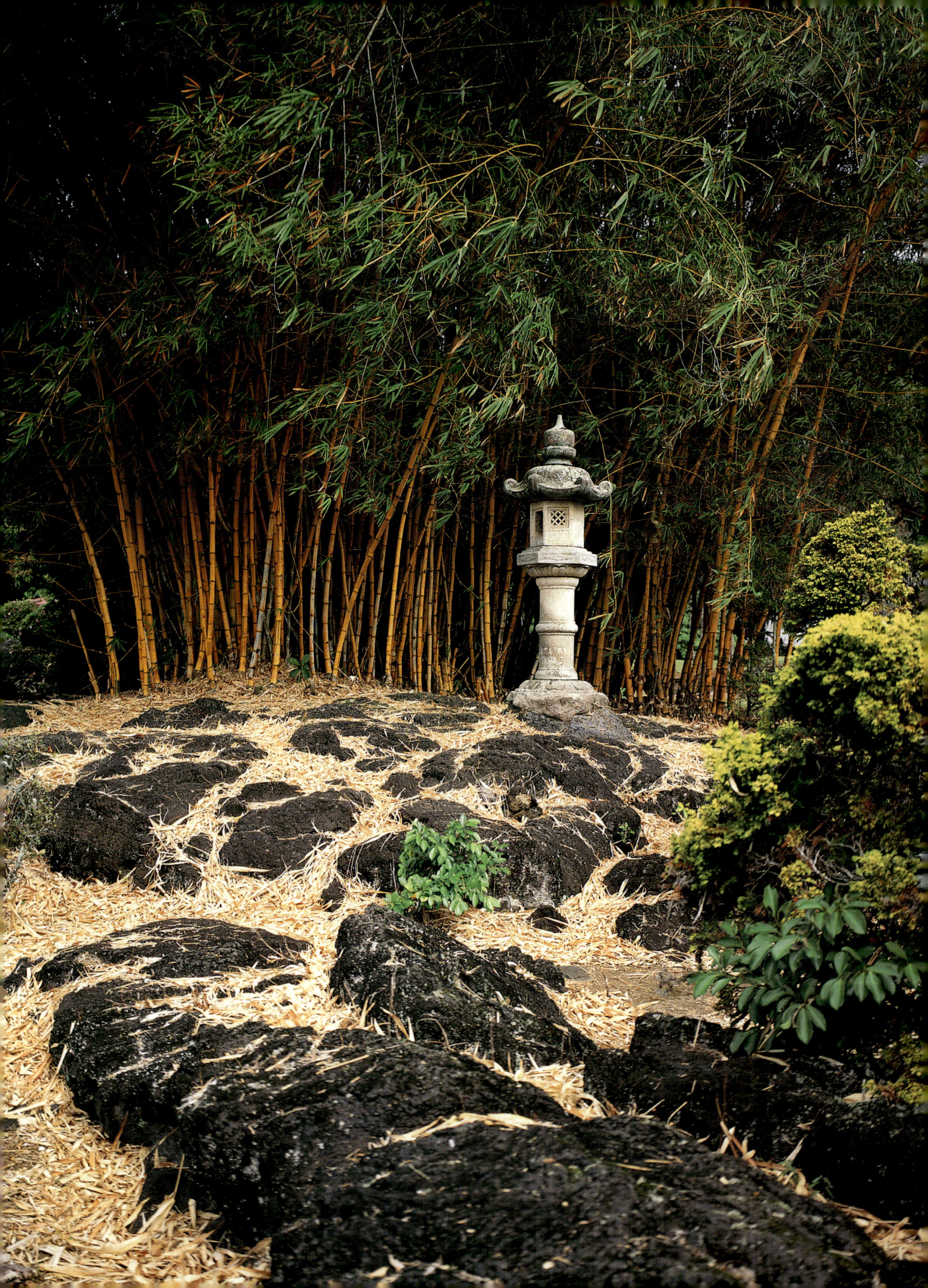

◁ Liliuokalani Gardens are named for Hawaii's last queen. A thirty-acre park situated in downtown Hilo on the Big Island, the gardens comprise the largest formal Japanese garden outside of Tokyo.
▽ One of Hawaii's green sea turtles uses its front and rear limbs to swim gracefully over the coral reef. While adults can weigh up to 500 pounds, this adolescent turtle is about three feet long and two feet across. Sea turtles, unlike land turtles and tortoises, cannot retract their heads into their shells.
▷ ▷ A traffic sign stands alone amid a lava flow, trying vainly to request order where none can exist.

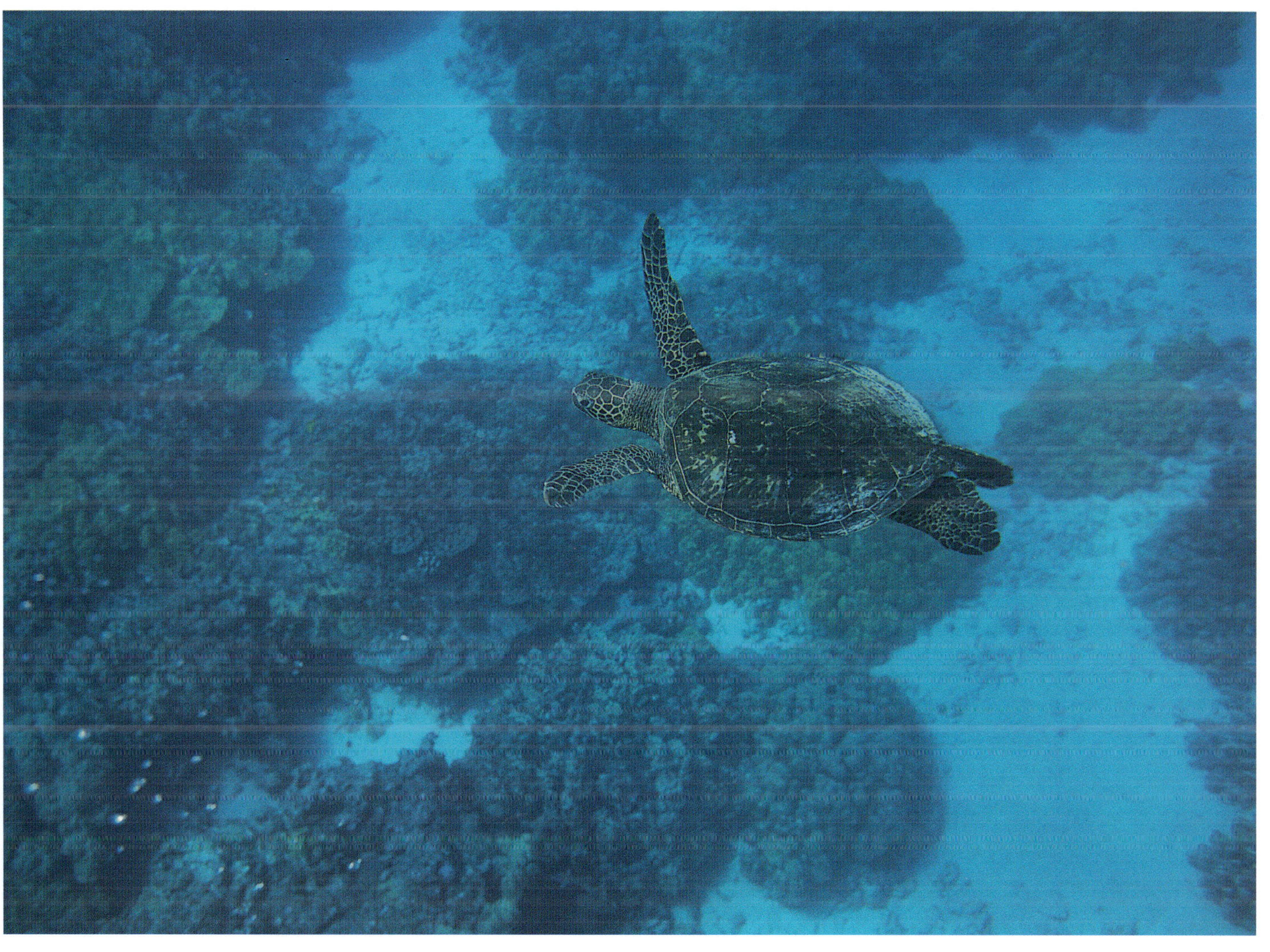

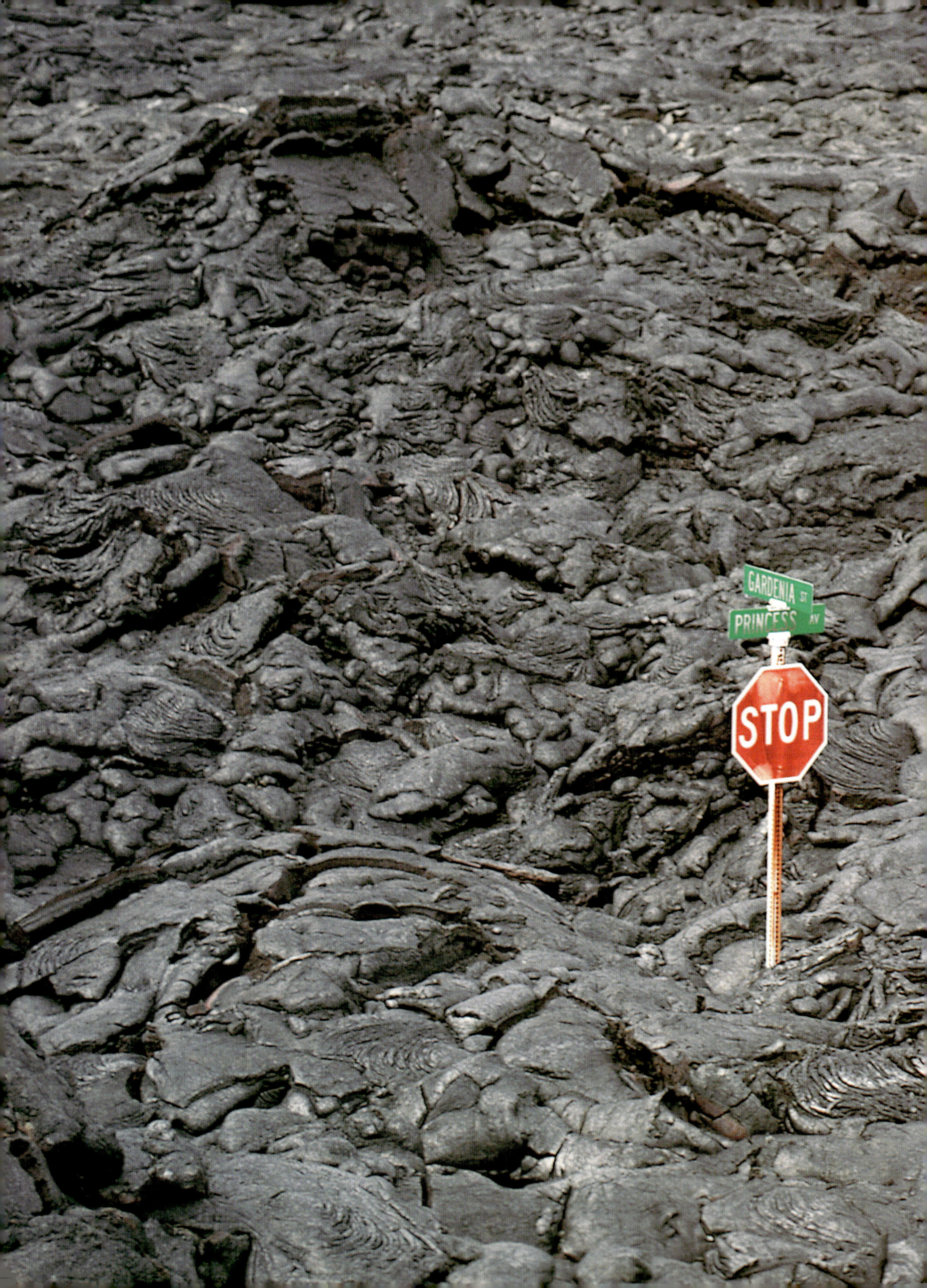
GARDENIA ST
PRINCESS AV
STOP

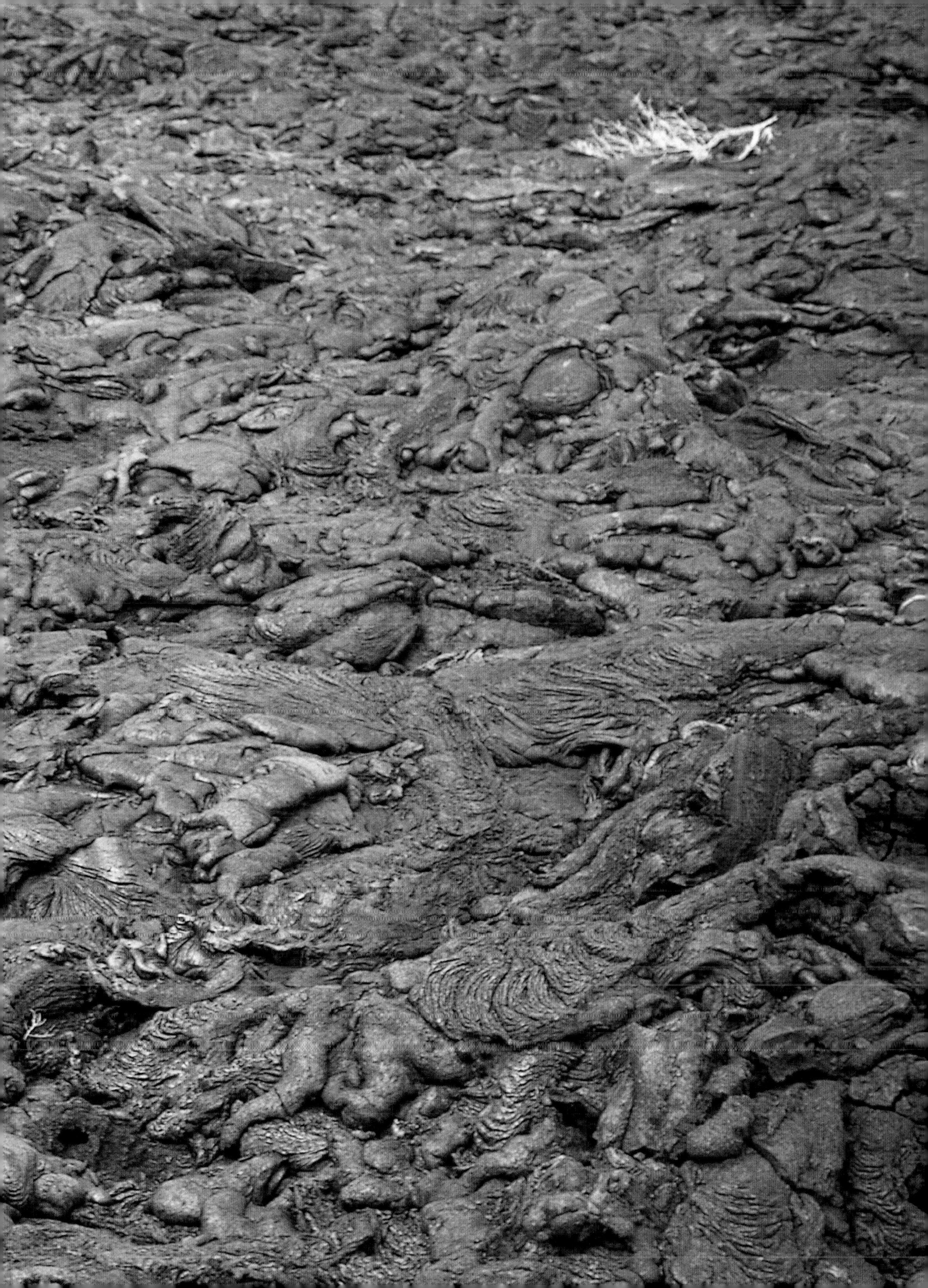

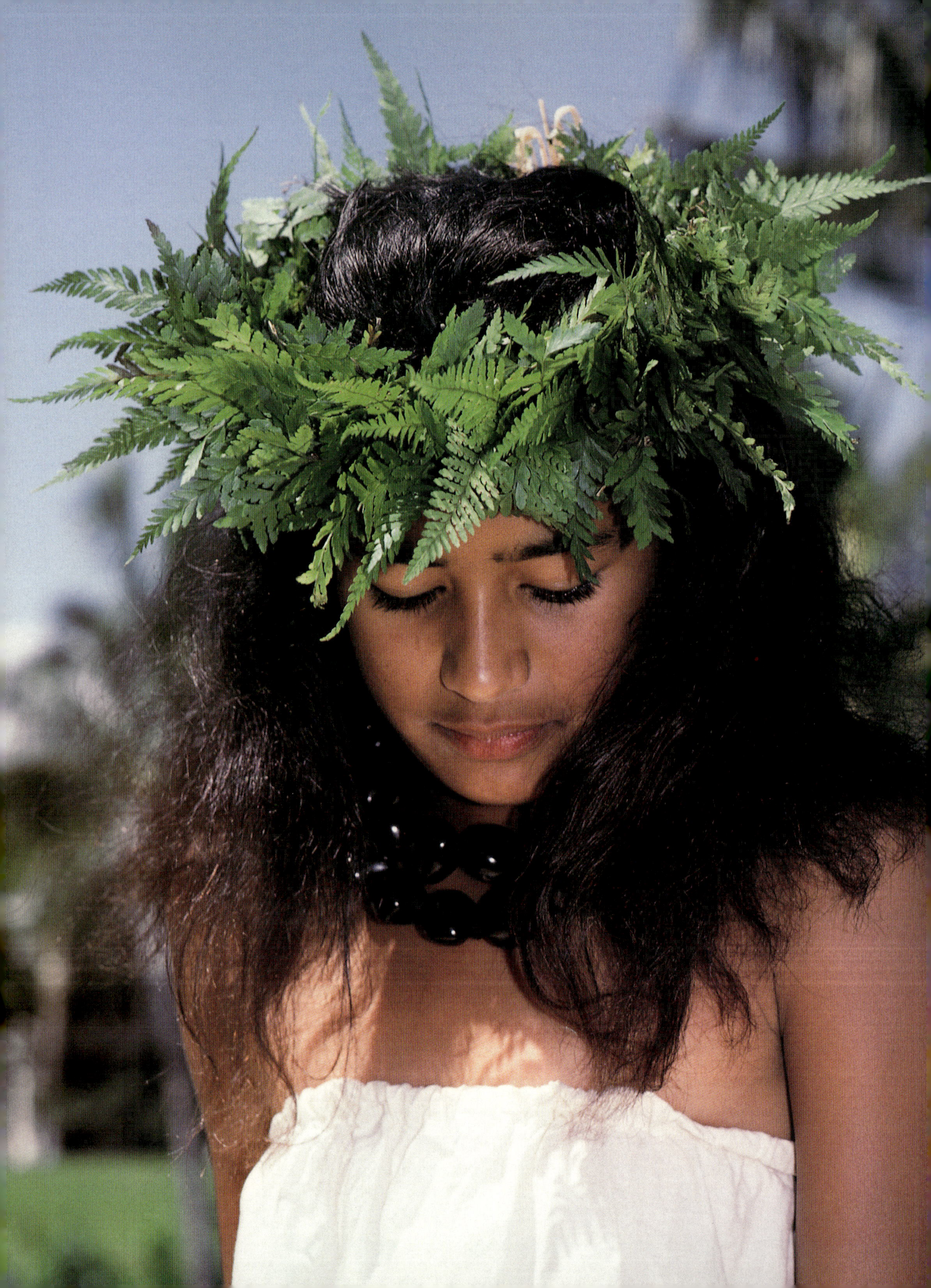

◁ Wearing a *haku* head lei made of ferns and a black kukui nut necklace, a young hula girl displays the sweet beauty of the Hawaiians. There is a renaissance of hula and other aspects of ancient Hawaiian culture.

▽ Although the islands began as barren lava rock, today they abound with flora and fauna. Many plants have been imported, beginning when the first Polynesians brought along what they needed to survive.

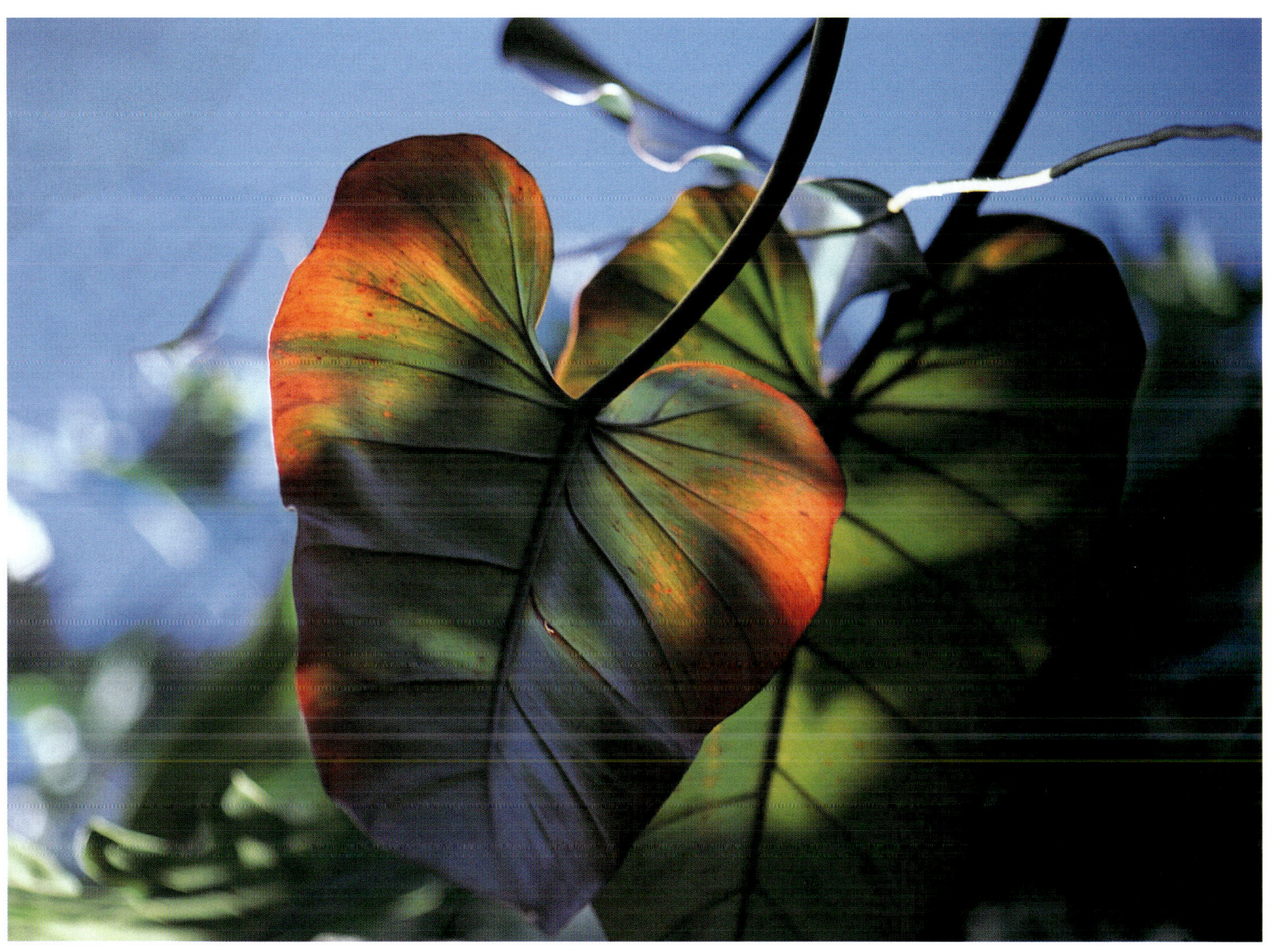

▽ A helicopter hovers above flowing red-hot lava of Kilauea Volcano at the Big Island's Volcano National Park. The surface of the lava cools and hardens quickly, forming a crust of rock. At times, the molten lava inside this rocky crust breaks a hole and flows through, leaving a huge lava cave or tunnel behind.
▷ Located on the leeward side of the Big Island, the quaint fishing town of Kailea-Kona is synonymous with great coffee, sunshine, and big game fishing. Alii Drive is a two-mile strip of tourist shops and restaurants.

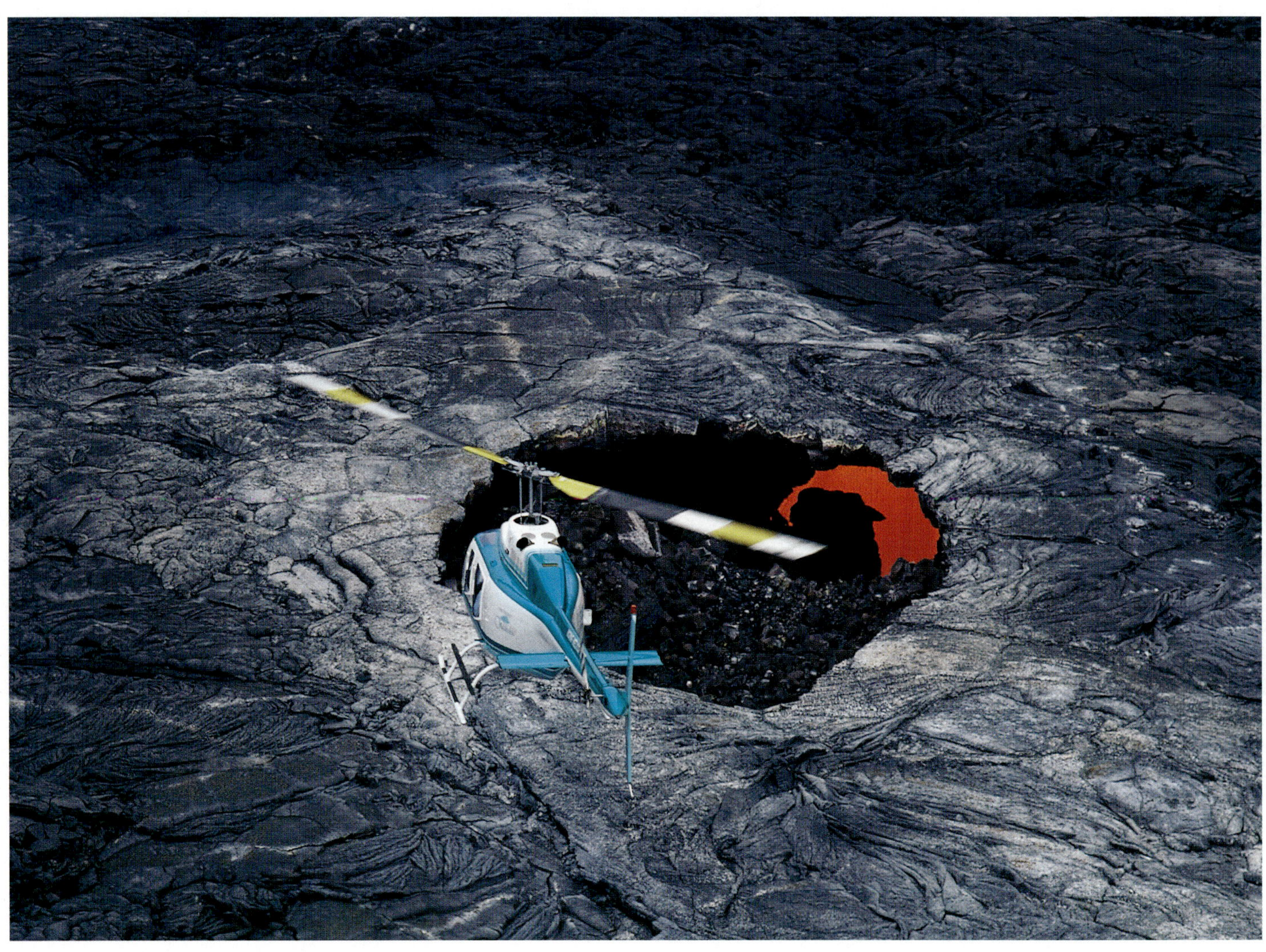

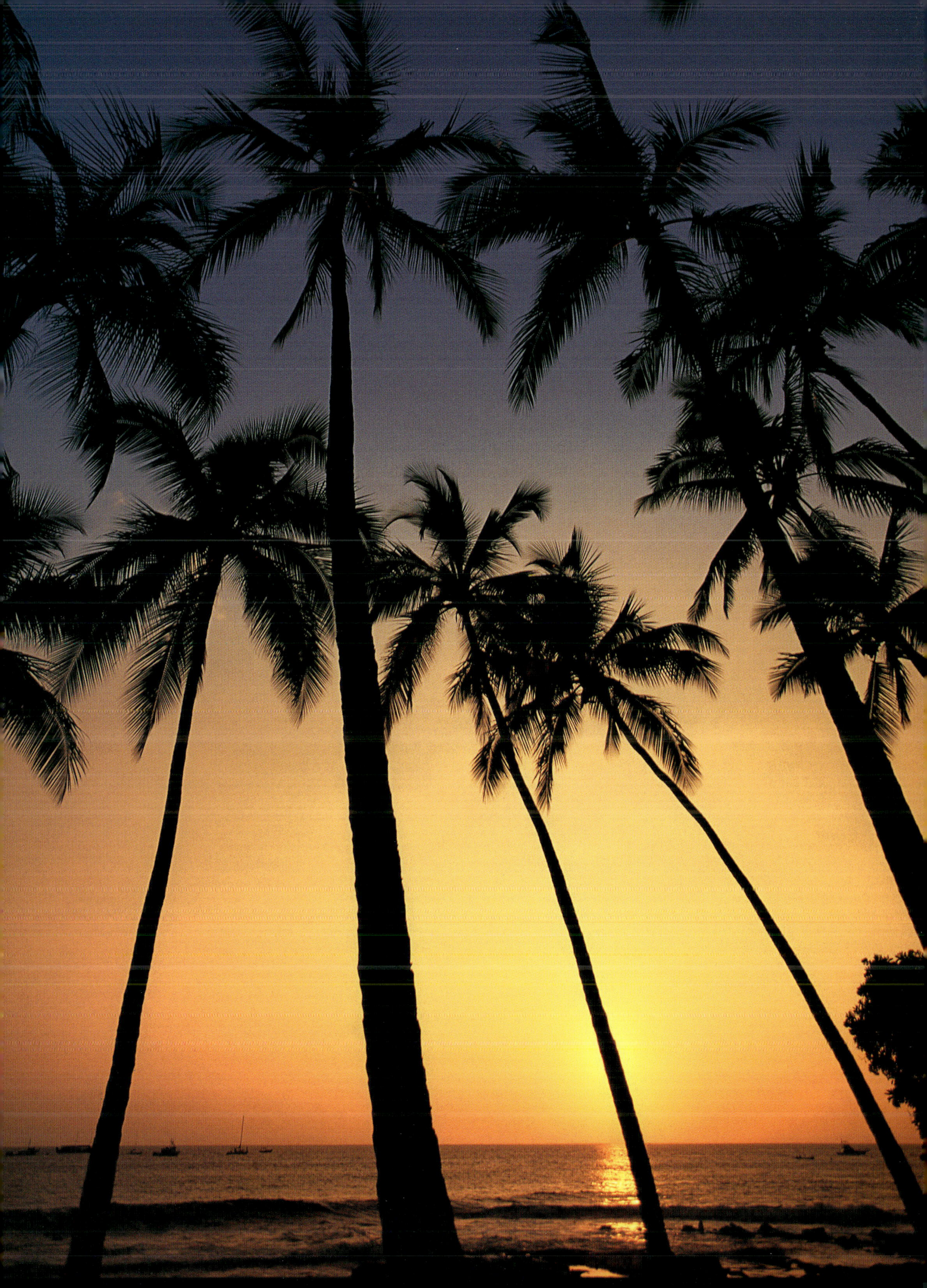

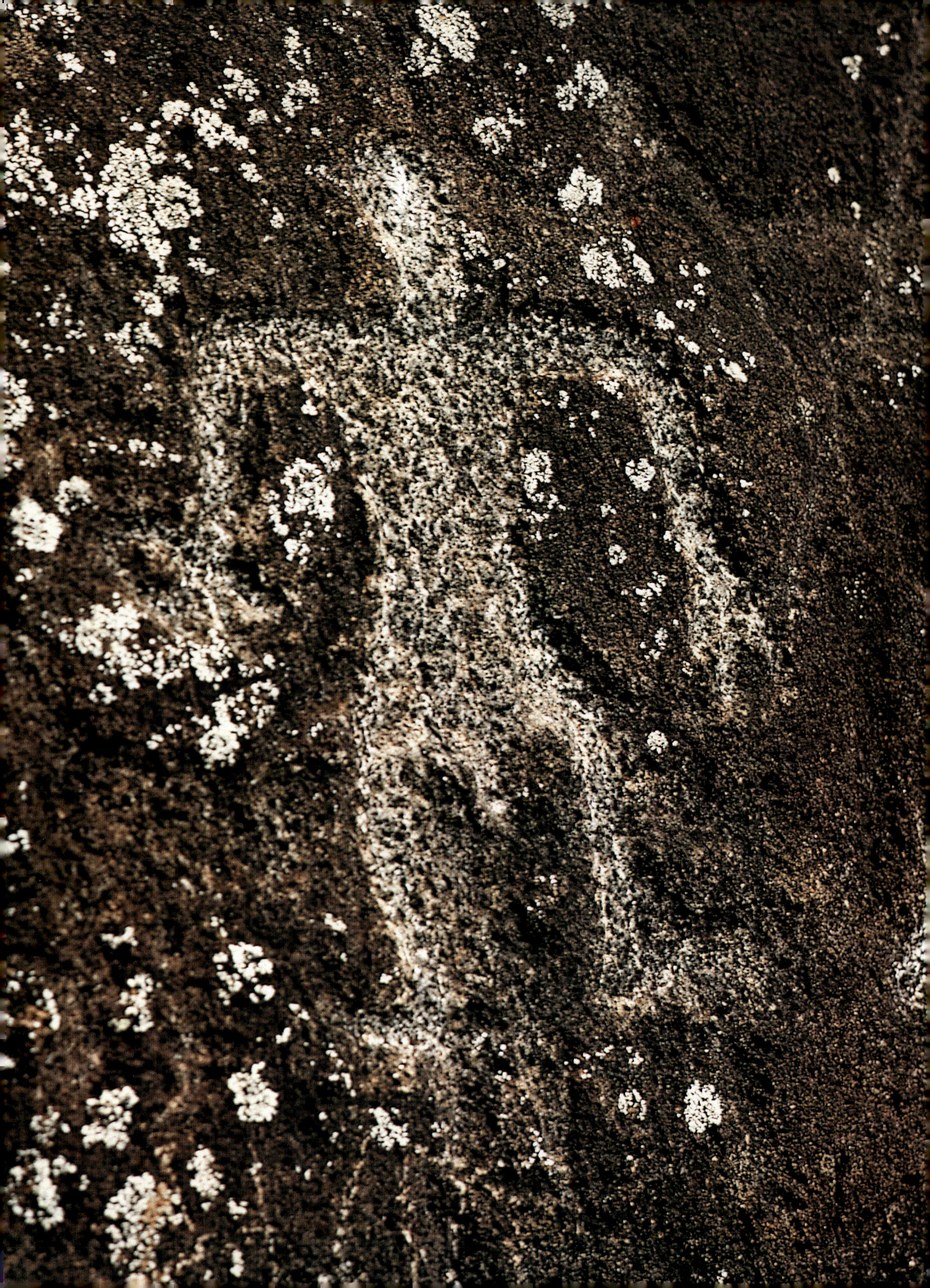

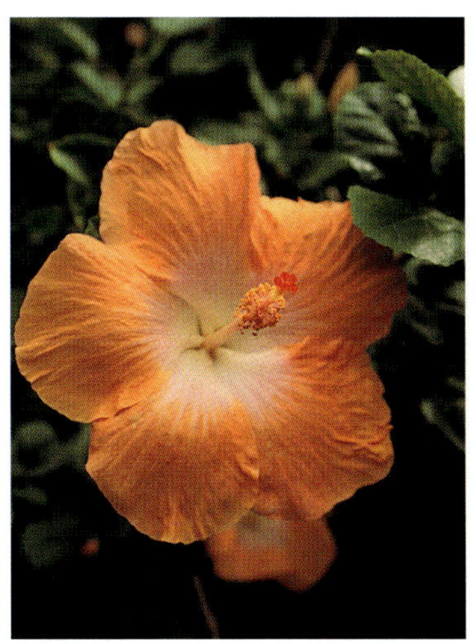

Lanai, Molokai, & Niihau

LANAI. The island of Lanai was sparsely populated until the 1920s when James Dole turned it into a prosperous pineapple operation. At the peak of production they shipped around a million pineapples a day. Today, only a few acres are grown, fulfilling the needs of the island's two world-class hotels. California investor David Murdock bought controlling interest of Lanai and built Manele Bay Hotel, overlooking gorgeous Hulopoe Beach, and the Lodge at Koele, nestled majestically inland among the Norfolk pines.

MOLOKAI. Among the remote valleys of Molokai, it is said the voices of Hawaiian Kahunas are still heard chanting ancient legends. This is where the Hawaiian spirit of *Ohana* and the hula were born. Molokai is a refuge from the flash and dash of tourism, big business, and commercial development. It has beautiful beaches, spectacular vistas, mule rides into the haunting leper colony at Kalapapa, and a quiet pace of life. Molokai is one of the last genuine Hawaiian places.

NIIHAU. Off Kauai's shore lies the tiny island of Niihau, Hawaii's most mysterious, private place. In 1864 Eliza Sinclair, daughter of a wealthy Scottish merchant, purchased the island from King Kamehameha V. Her descendants, the Robinsons, still own the island. Their desire for privacy and appreciation for Hawaiian culture prompted them to limit island access to residents and invited guests. About three hundred pure Hawaiians live in a village similar to that of their ancestors.

◁ *Luahiwa Petroglyph Field lies just outside of Lanai City.*
△ *Hibiscus flowers flourish throughout the islands.*
▷ ▷ *A cross honors the 11,000 who died of leprosy on Molokai.*

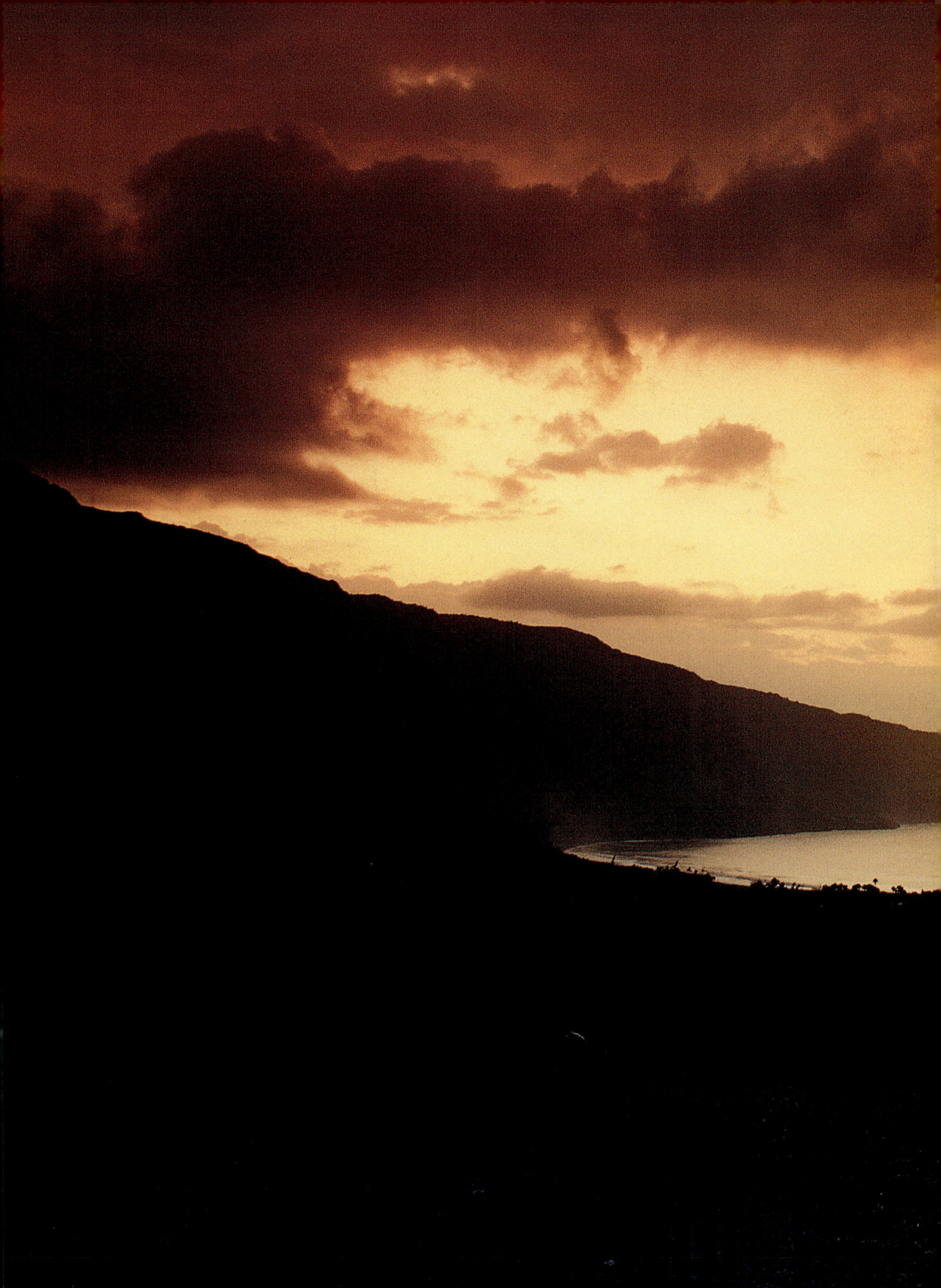

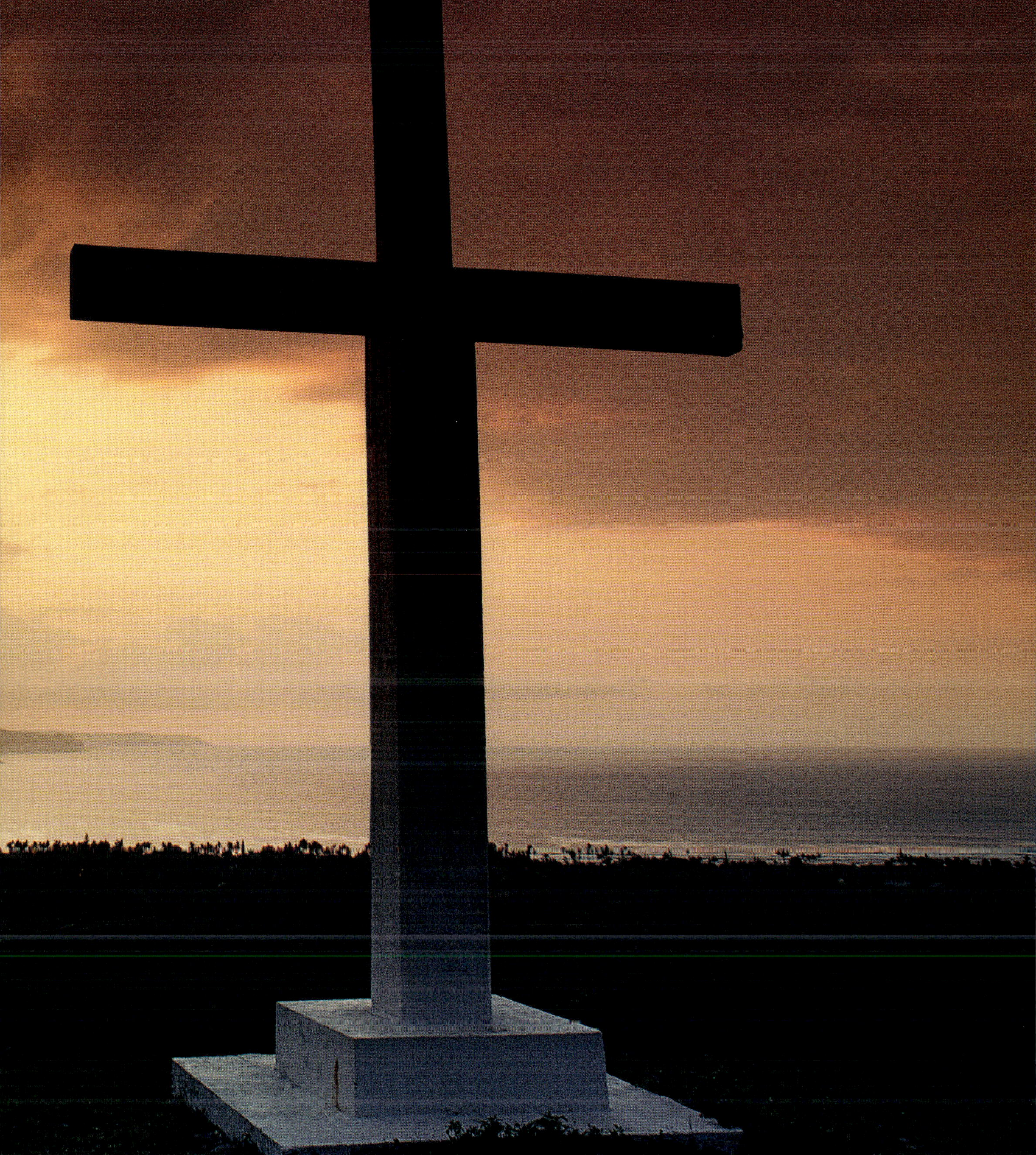

▽ Lanai has huge stretches of uncrowded sandy beaches, and Hulopoe is the best of these. Set on a bluff overlooking this golden-sand beach, the Manele Bay Hotel is a stunningly beautiful destination. This luxurious Hawaiian retreat combines with the island's best swimming, snorkeling, and tanning beach to create a perfect vacation getaway. ▷ Fishing is good off Shipwreck Beach, located along the Kalohi Channel, which separates the islands of Lanai and Molokai.

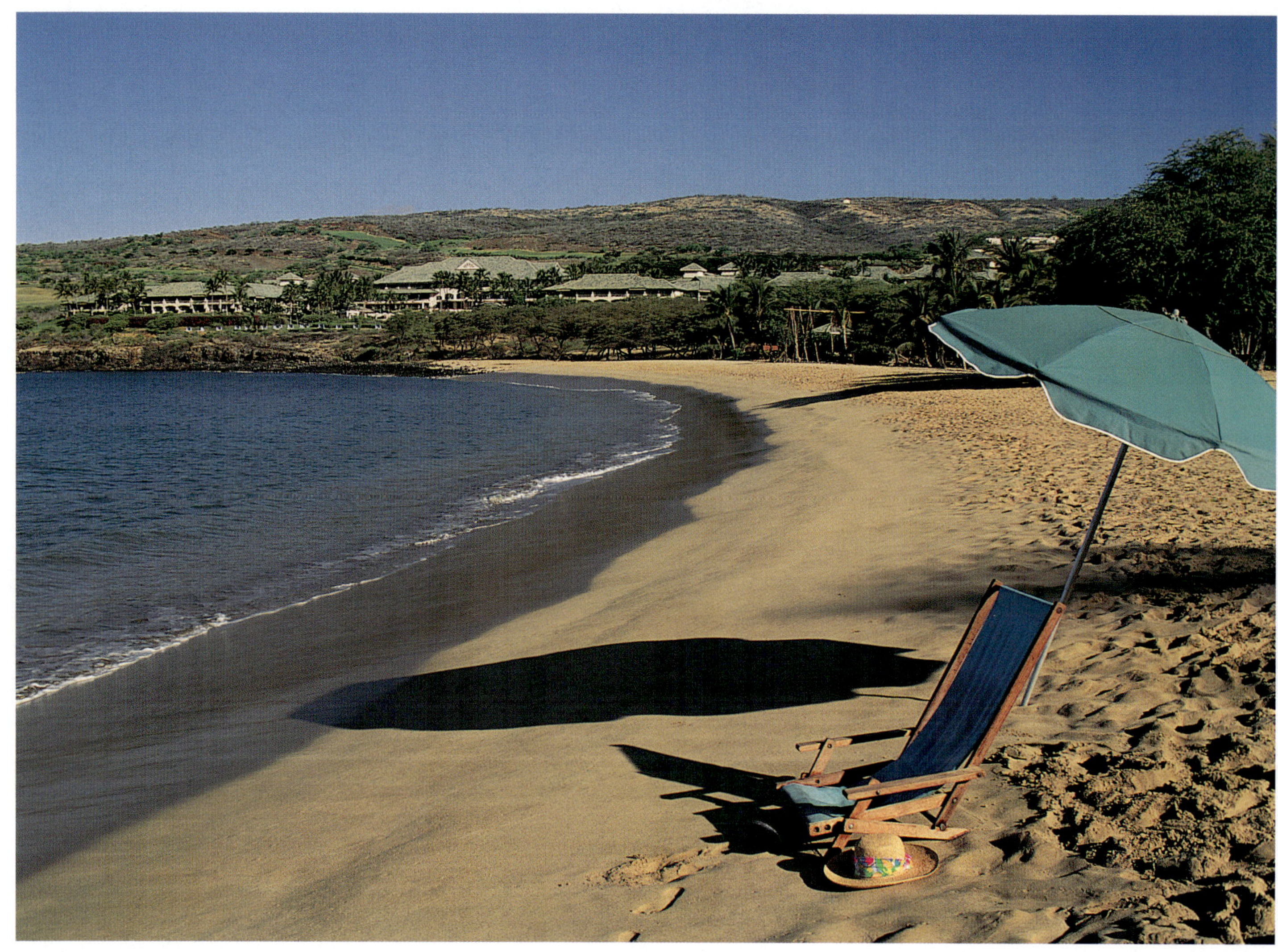

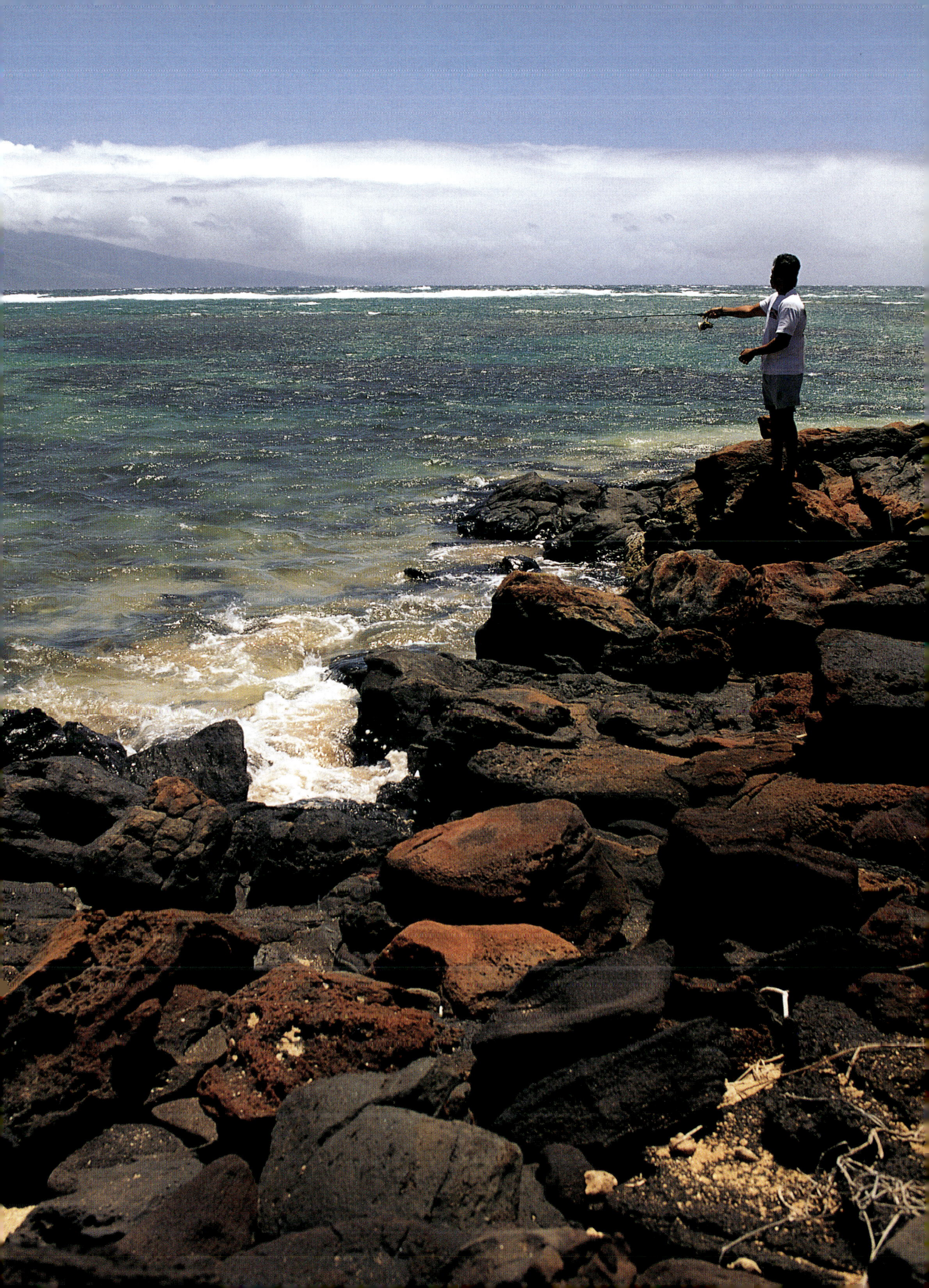

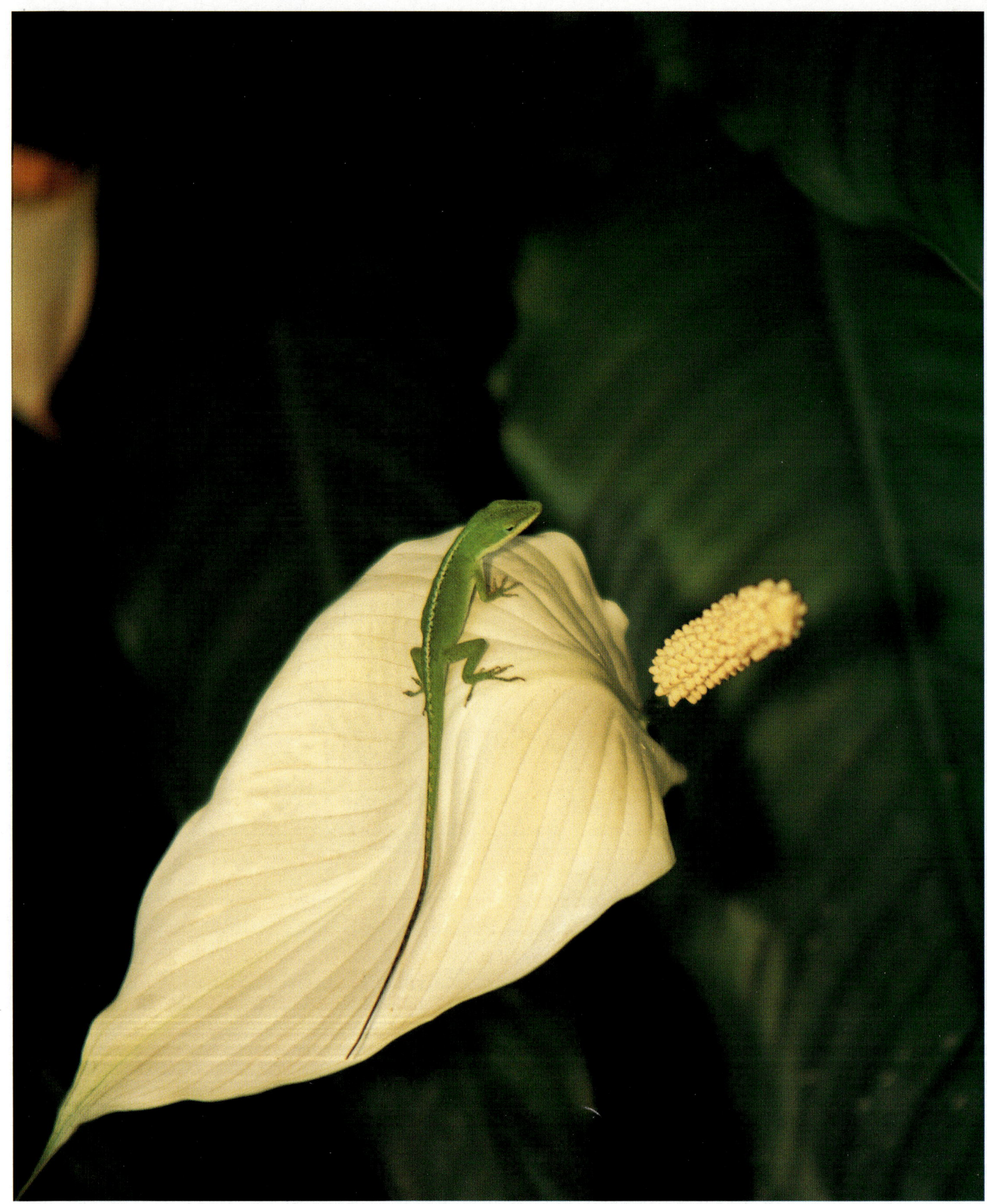

△ A small green anole, a soft-skinned, harmless lizard, sits on a Mauna Loa flower.
▷ Garden of the Gods glows with earthen tints of red, burnt orange, ochre, and yellow, contrasted with the brilliant green of the striking yucca plants.

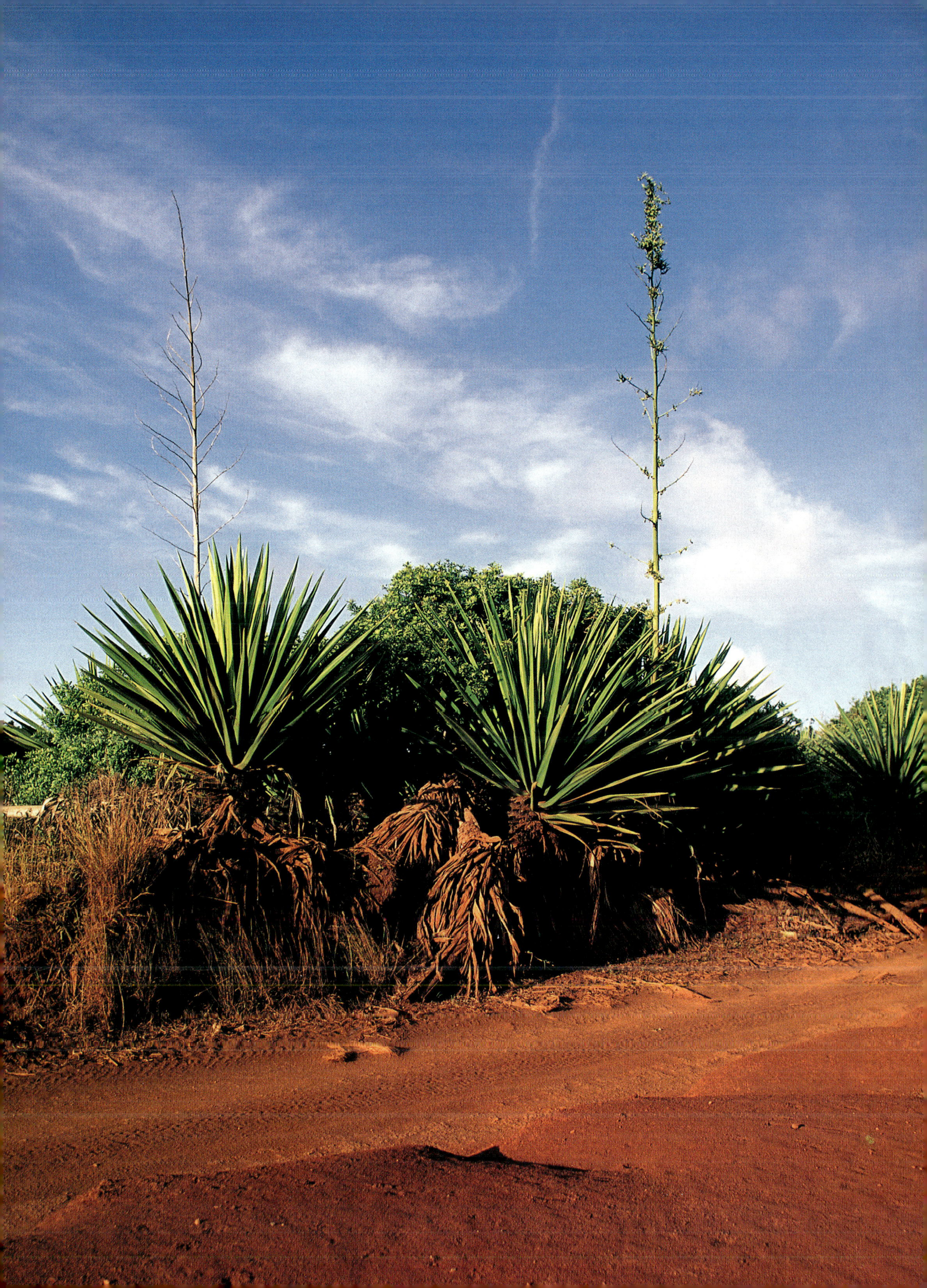

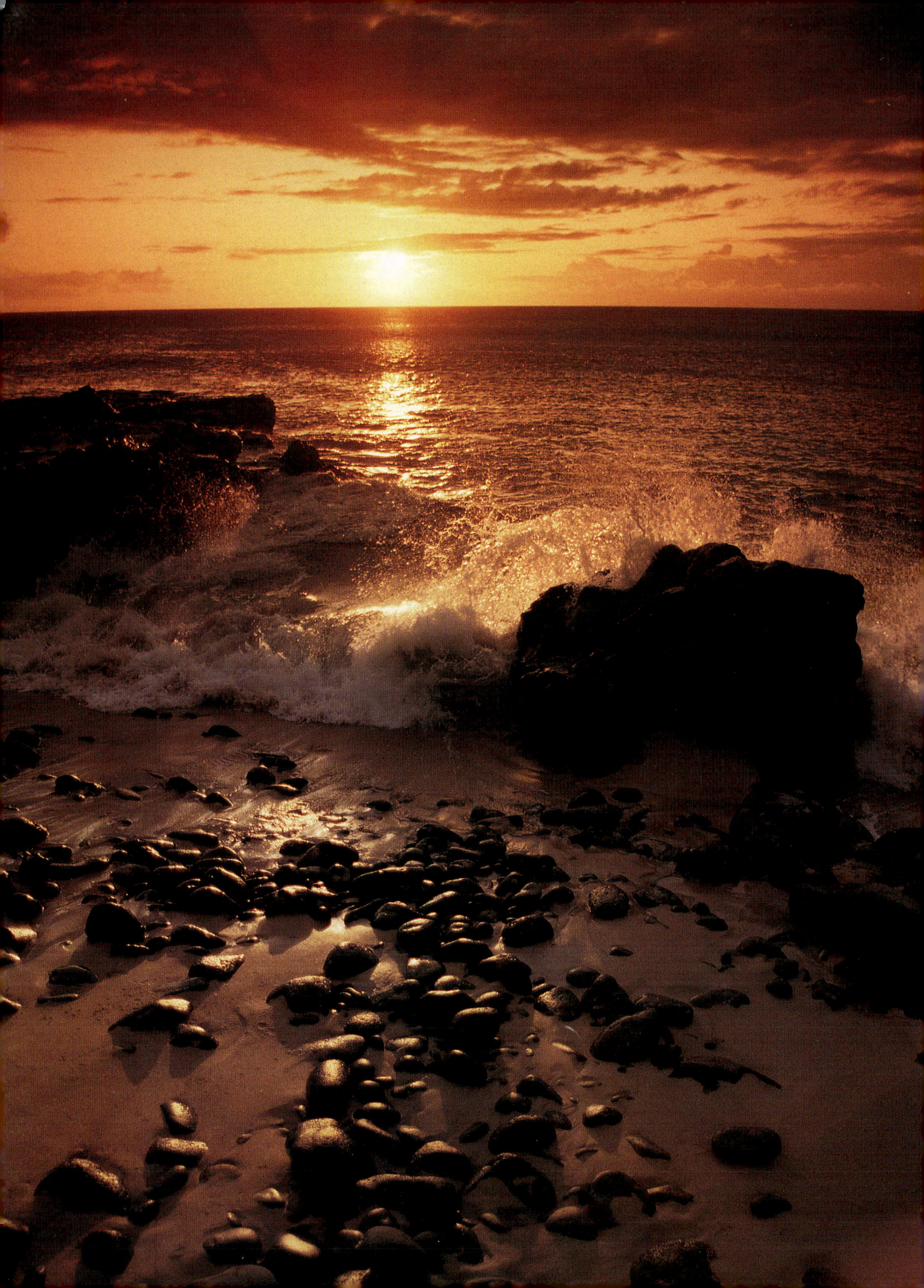

◁ With golden sands three miles long and a hundred yards wide, Papahaku Beach is one of Hawaii's largest and prettiest. Sunbathing and beach combing are great, but with an undercurrent that is nicknamed the "Oahu Express," swimming in these waters is only for the strong and experienced. ▽ *Kaiolohia Bay*, which means "choppy or changing sea," is commonly called Shipwreck Beach because of the rusting hulk of a tanker that ran aground on Lanai's coral reef more than fifty years ago.

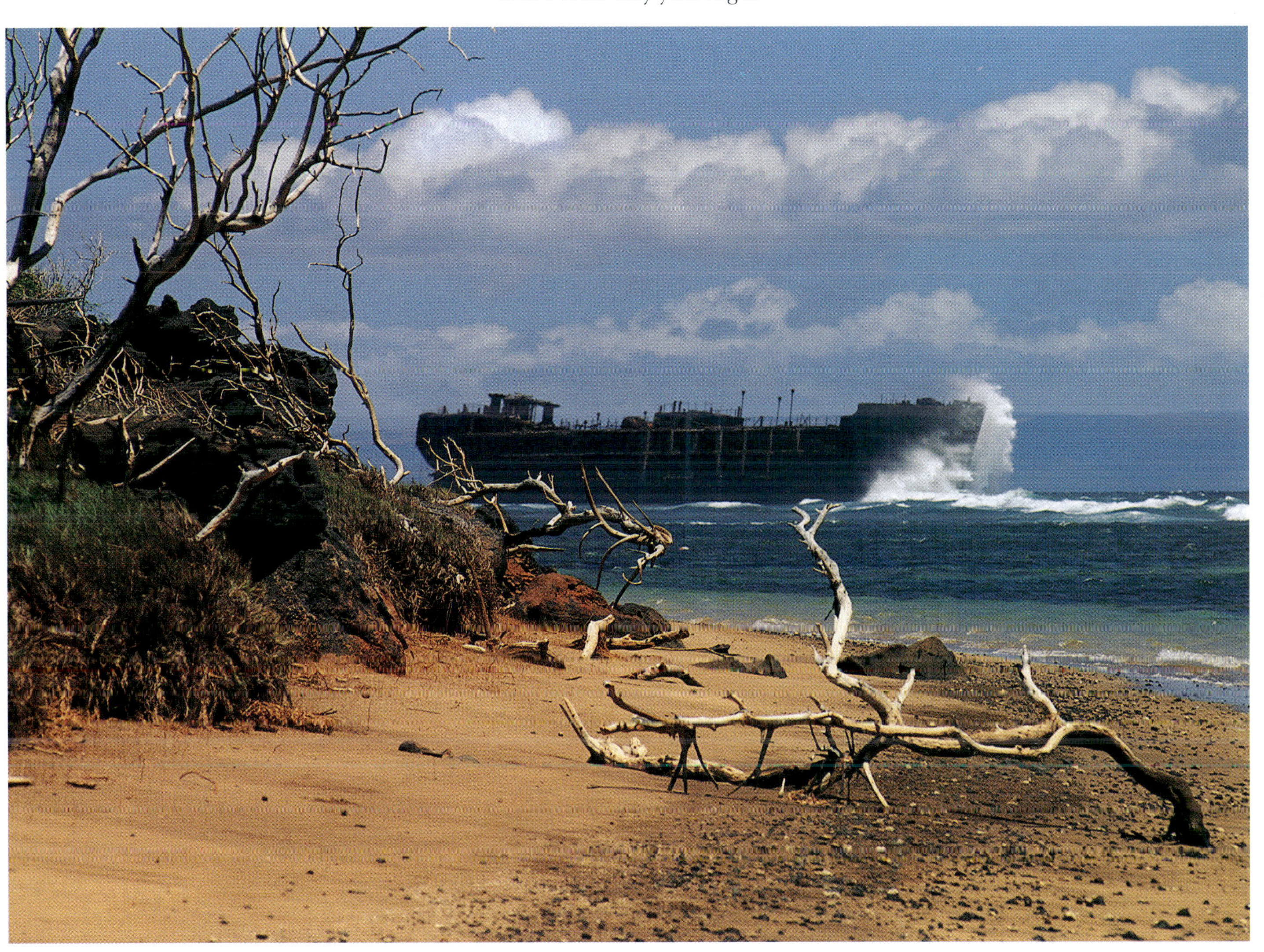

▽ Called the "Forbidden Island," Niihau is a privately owned island just seventeen miles across the Kaulakahi Channel from Kauai's west side. It is the only island where Hawaiian is the primary language.

▷ A helicopter lands on the rugged coastline of Niihau, an island that has no airfield. Tourists who take the expensive trip are only allowed to visit a remote and uninhabited part of the island. The helicopter service was started to provide emergency medical care.

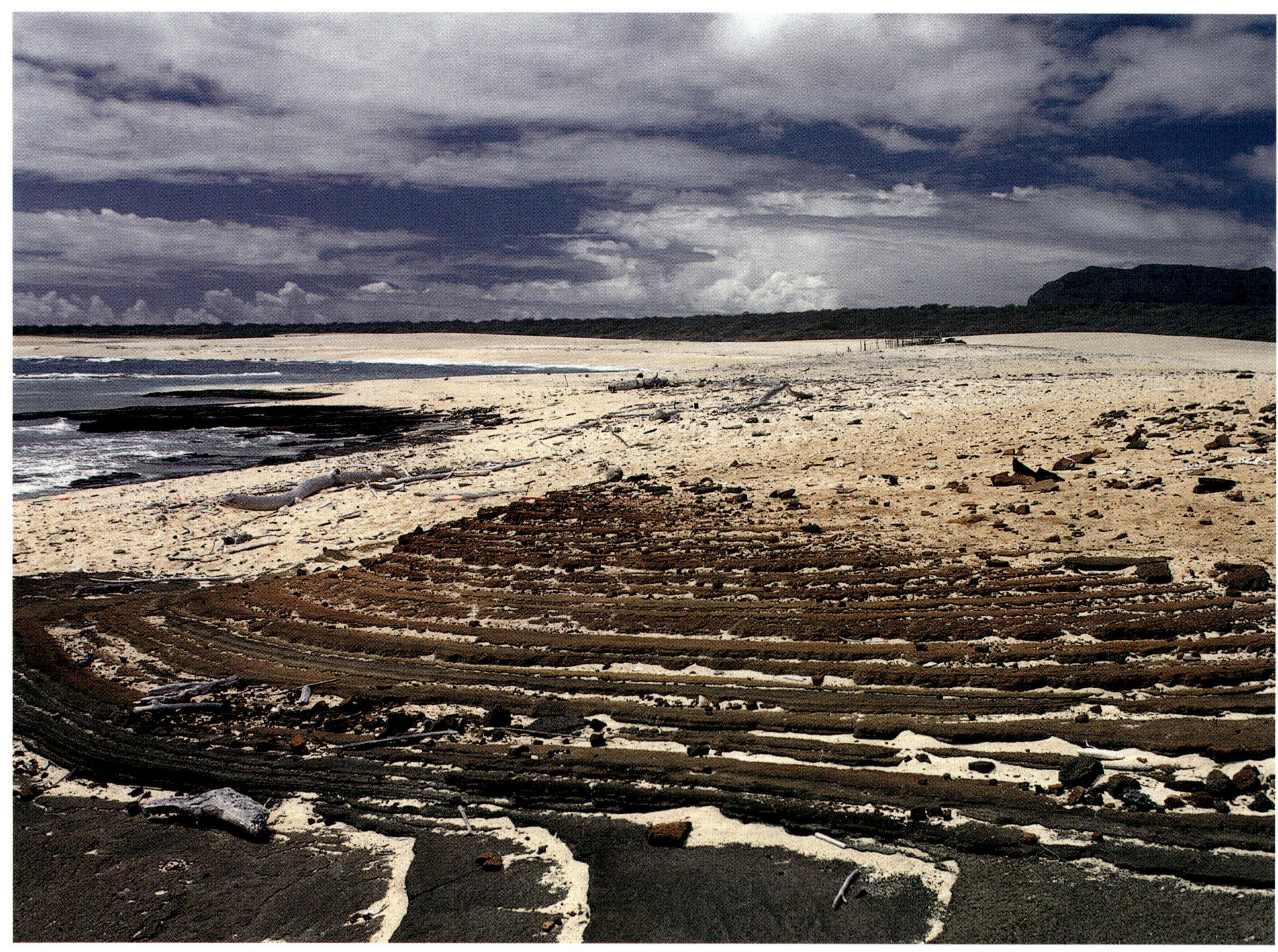

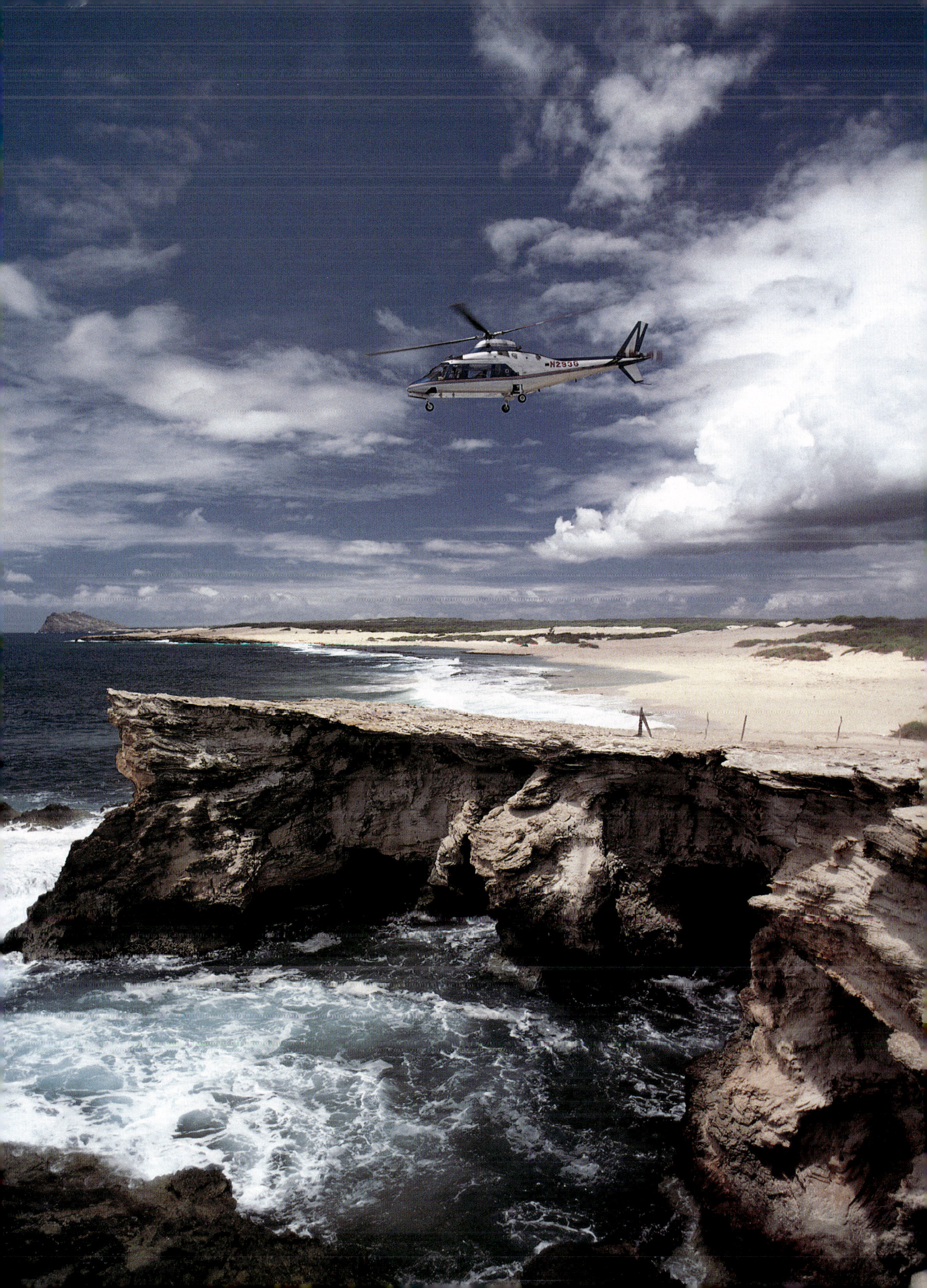
N293G

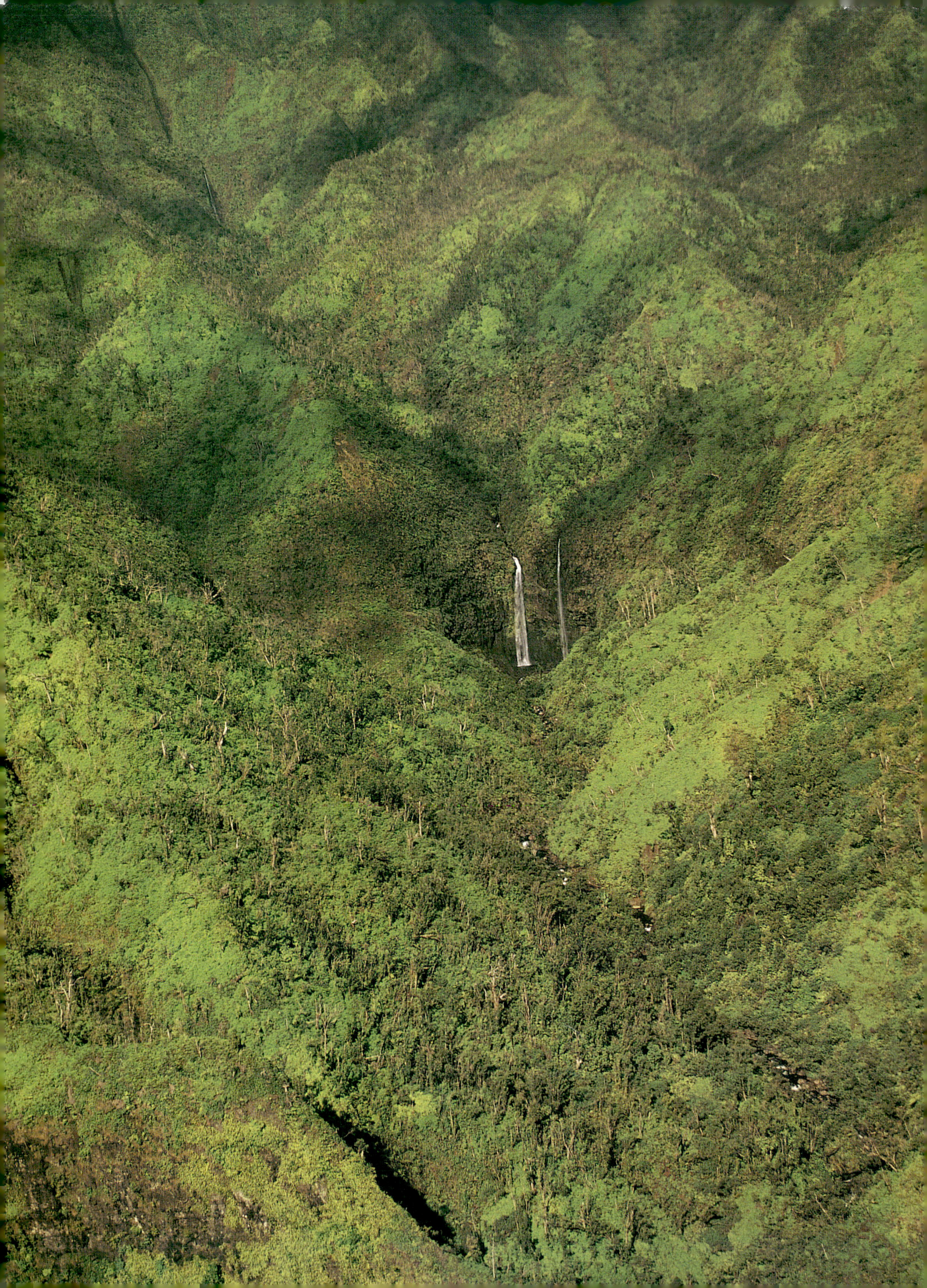

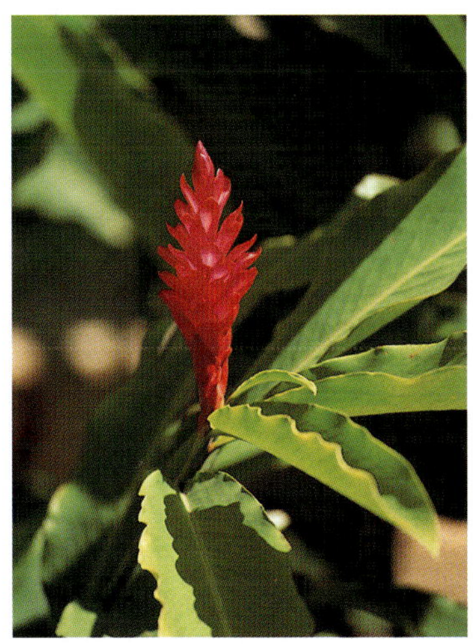

Kauai

When King Kamehameha united his kingdom by ruthless battles with the kings of Maui, Oahu, and the Big Island, Kauai successfully resisted. Following a generation of negotiations, threats, and even royal kidnapping, Kauai reluctantly became a semi-independent part of the sovereignty. Even so, the island's free spirit lives on.

Twenty million years after this oldest Hawaiian island was created, Kauai is a place of unusual beauty and character. Blessed with emerald rain forests, majestic cliffs and valleys, and lush tropical vegetation, it is called the "Garden Isle."

Captain James Cook encountered the Hawaiian Islands in 1778, dropping anchor on the coast of Kauai. He found a sleepy village of grass shacks and friendly people. Plentiful with exotic fruits, wild pigs, beautiful women, and balmy weather, it was the land of dreams.

Today, visitors find the same beautiful terrain and are greeted by descendants of the same friendly Hawaiians. Outsiders are drawn by the island's natural beauty, rather than by planned destination attractions and mega resorts.

Recently, Kauai has twice been devastated by hurricanes. Each time, the people and island have shown their true character, springing back better than before. Hawaiians call this strength of land and people working together the *Ohana*, or spirit of *Aloha*. While the *Ohana* is found throughout Hawaii, its presence is especially strong on the beautiful island of Kauai.

◁ *Waterfalls spill from cliffs within the Waimea Canyon.*
△ *A native of Malaya, red ginger blooms most of the year on Kauai.*
▷▷ *Up to 20-foot waves make surfing great on Kauai's North Shore.*

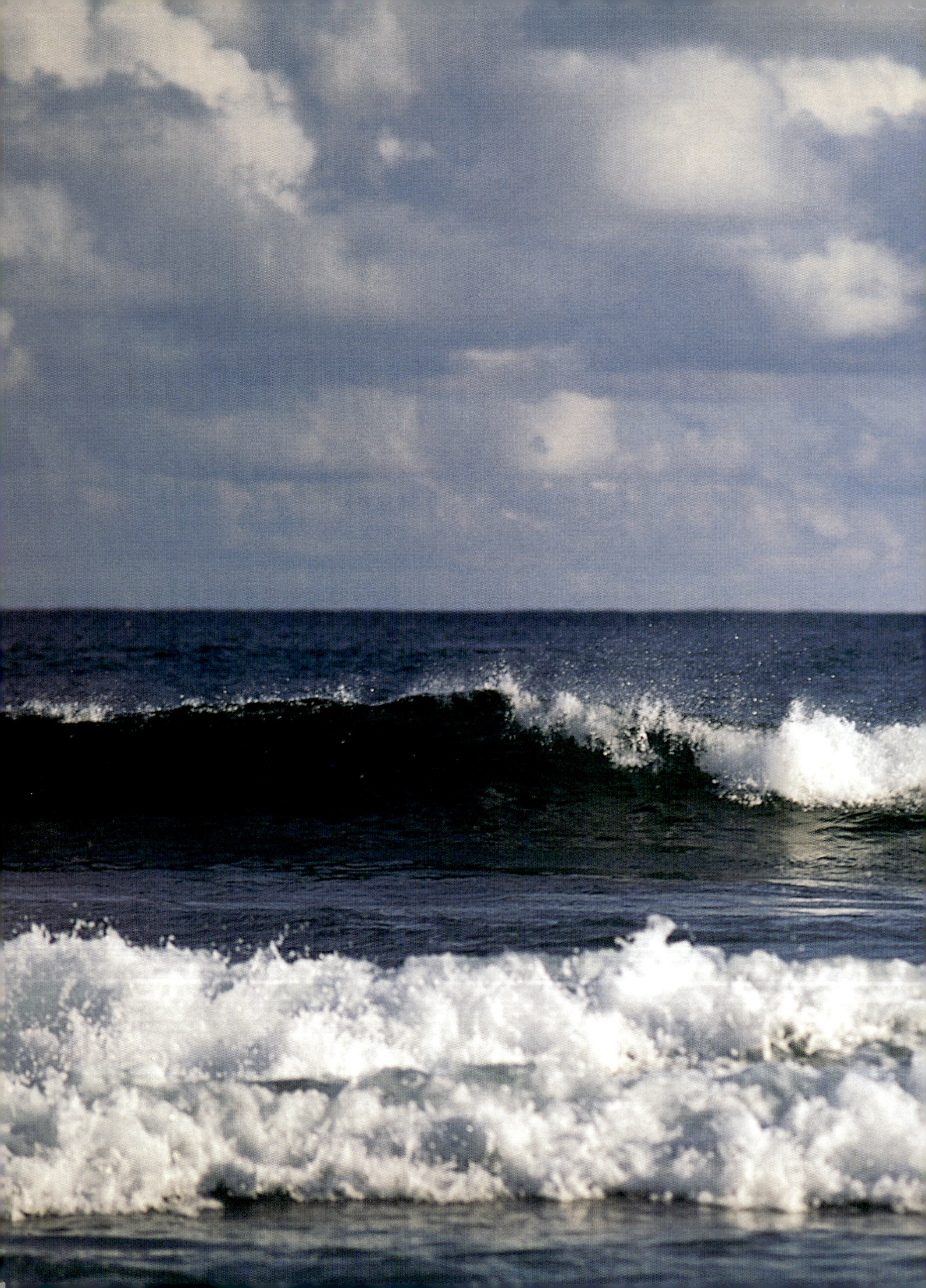

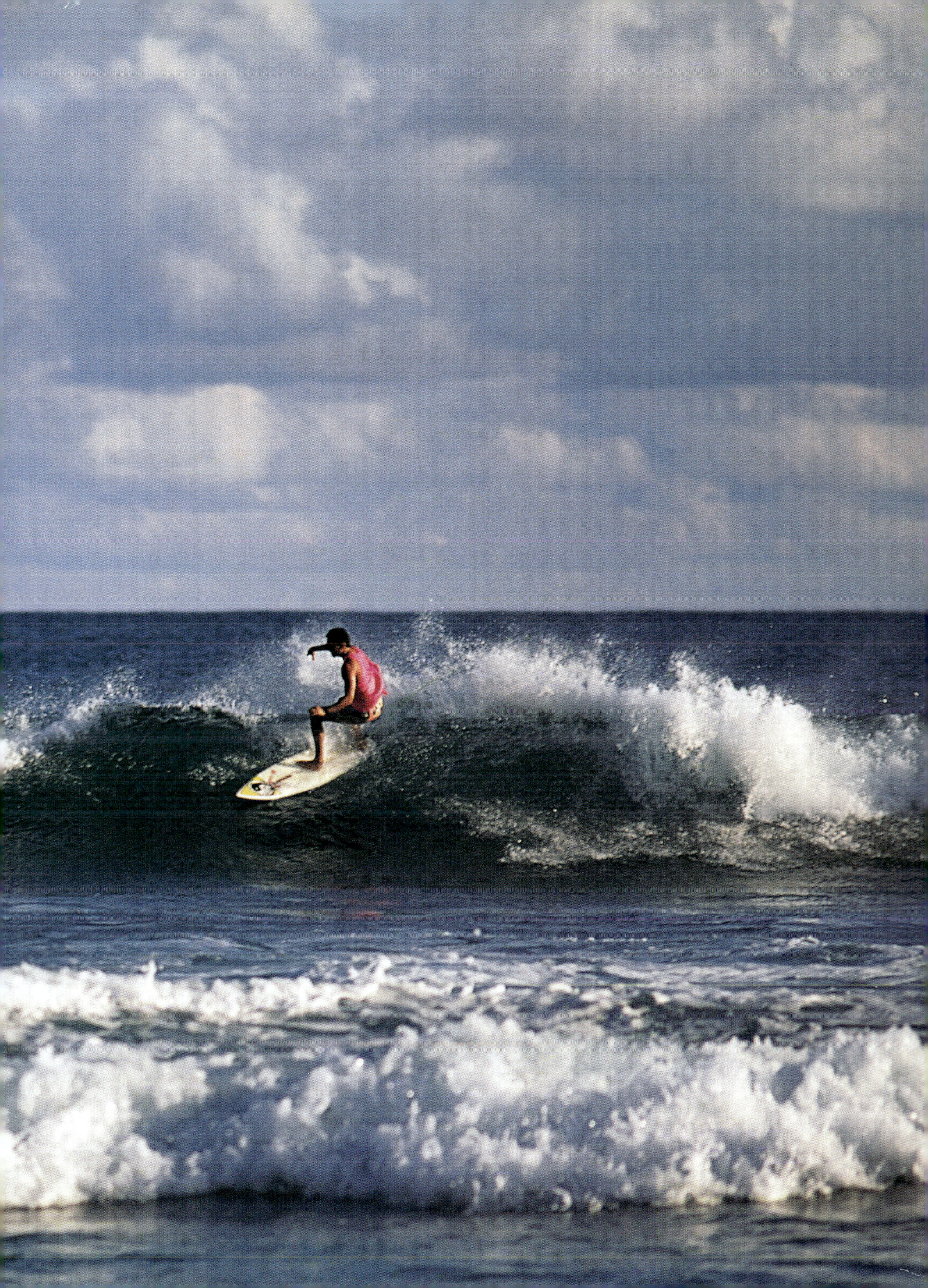

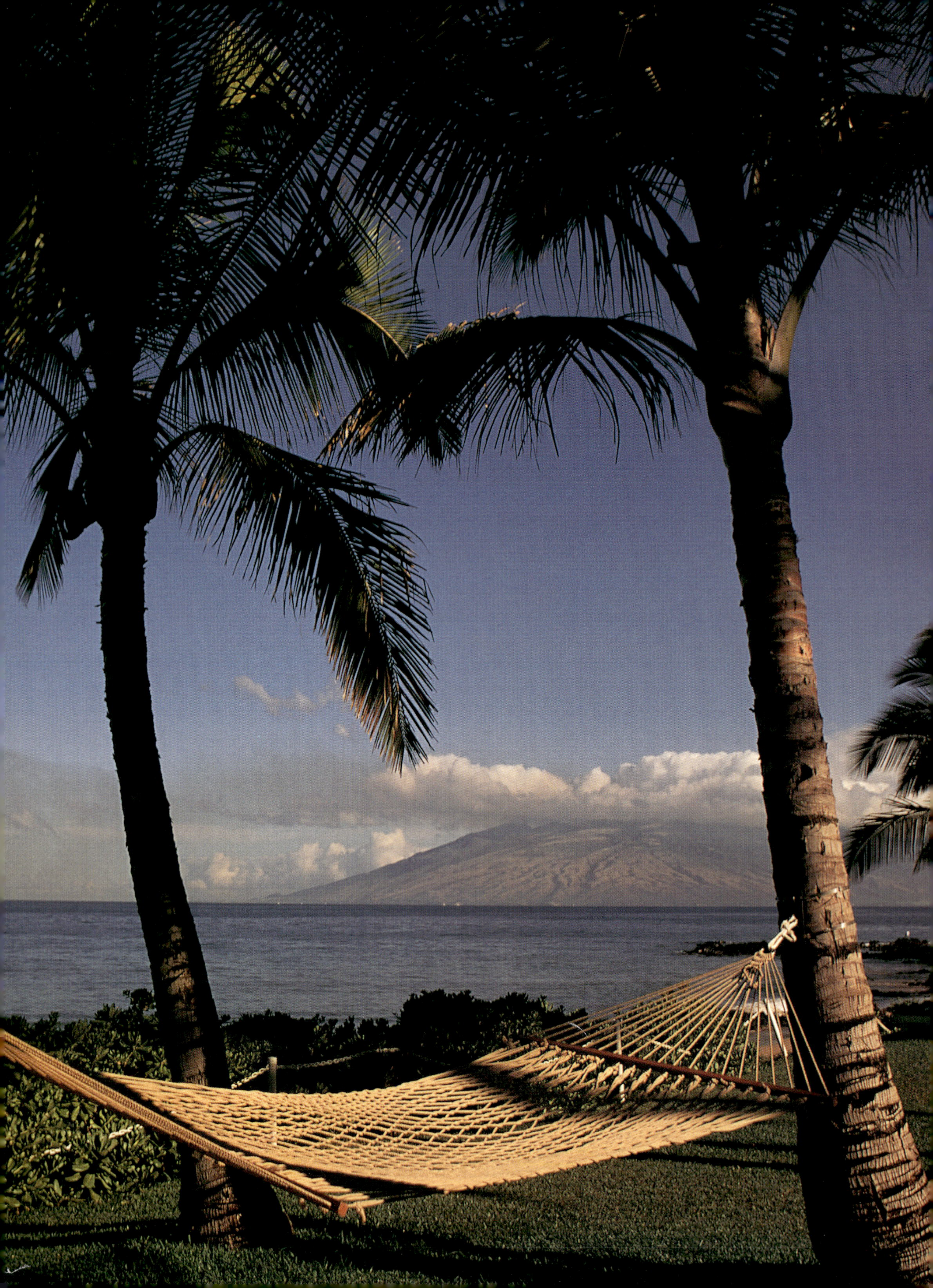

◁ A hammock strung between two palm trees is the perfect way to enjoy Hawaii. Blessed with sunshine, gentle trade winds, clear blue skies, and abundant natural beauty, Hawaii is one of the world's most beautiful treasures.
▽ Lumahai Beach, on Kauai's north side, is only two miles outside of Hanalei. This sandy beach is rarely crowded even though it gained fame by appearing in the movie *South Pacific.*

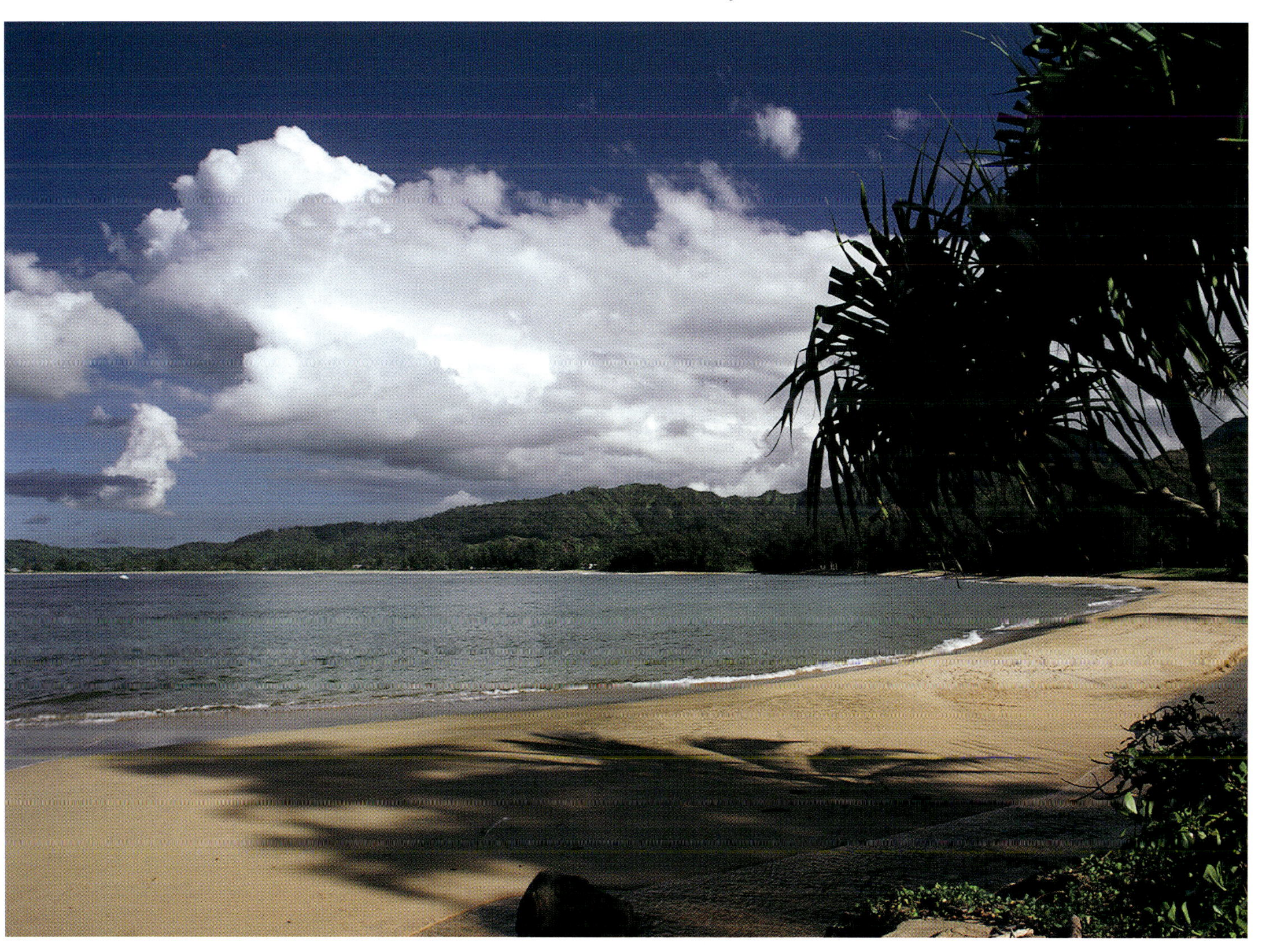

▽ A surfer takes a break between waves and enjoys the warm sunshine on Poipu Beach. Kauai's southernmost point is the sunny part of the island and an area of low-rise hotels.
▷ Taro grows in a field in the Hanalei Valley on the north side of Kauai. With the gentle Hanalei River cutting across, the Hanalei Valley is a patchwork of taro fields framed by green mountains and the beautiful Hanalei Bay.

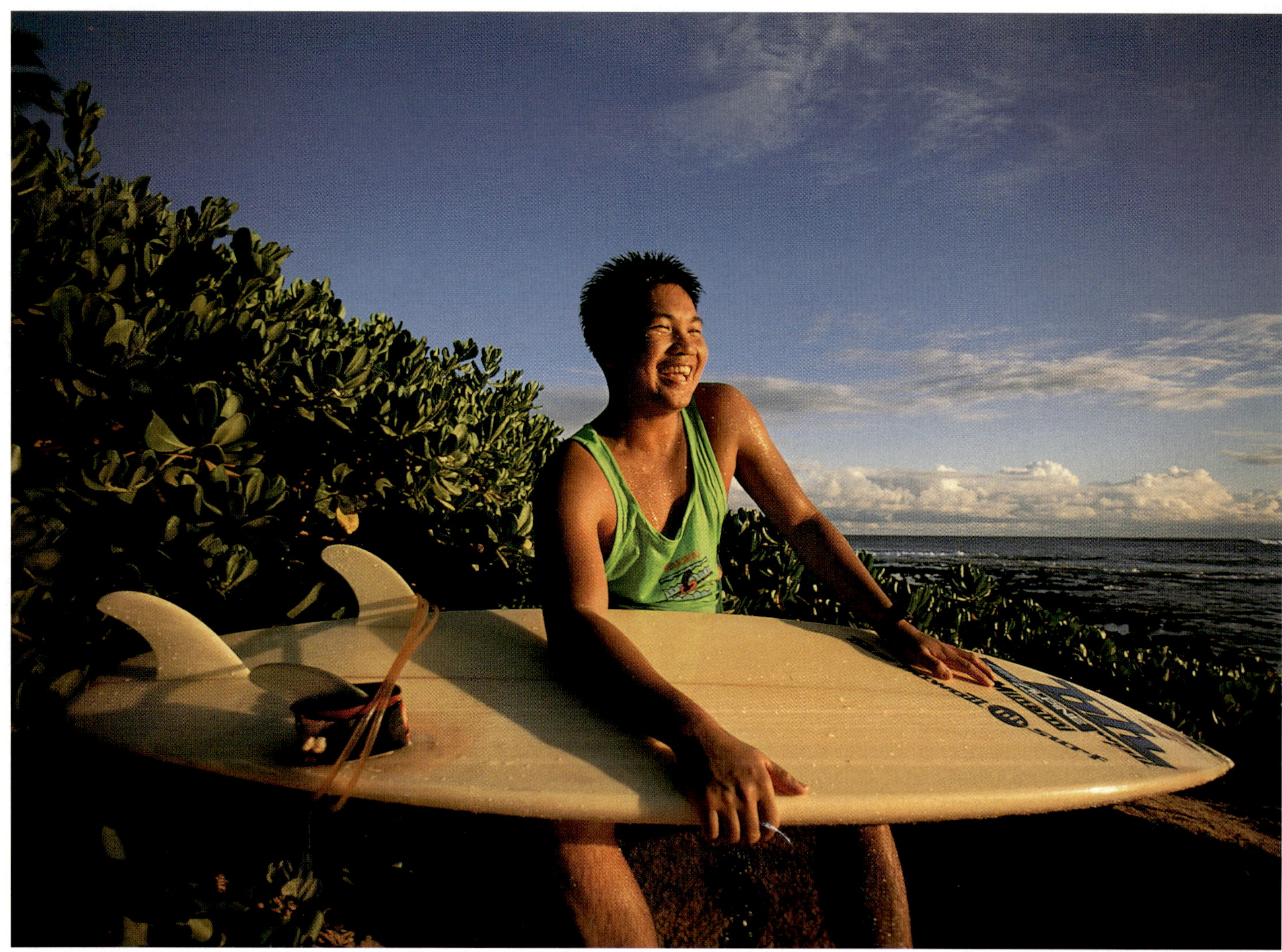

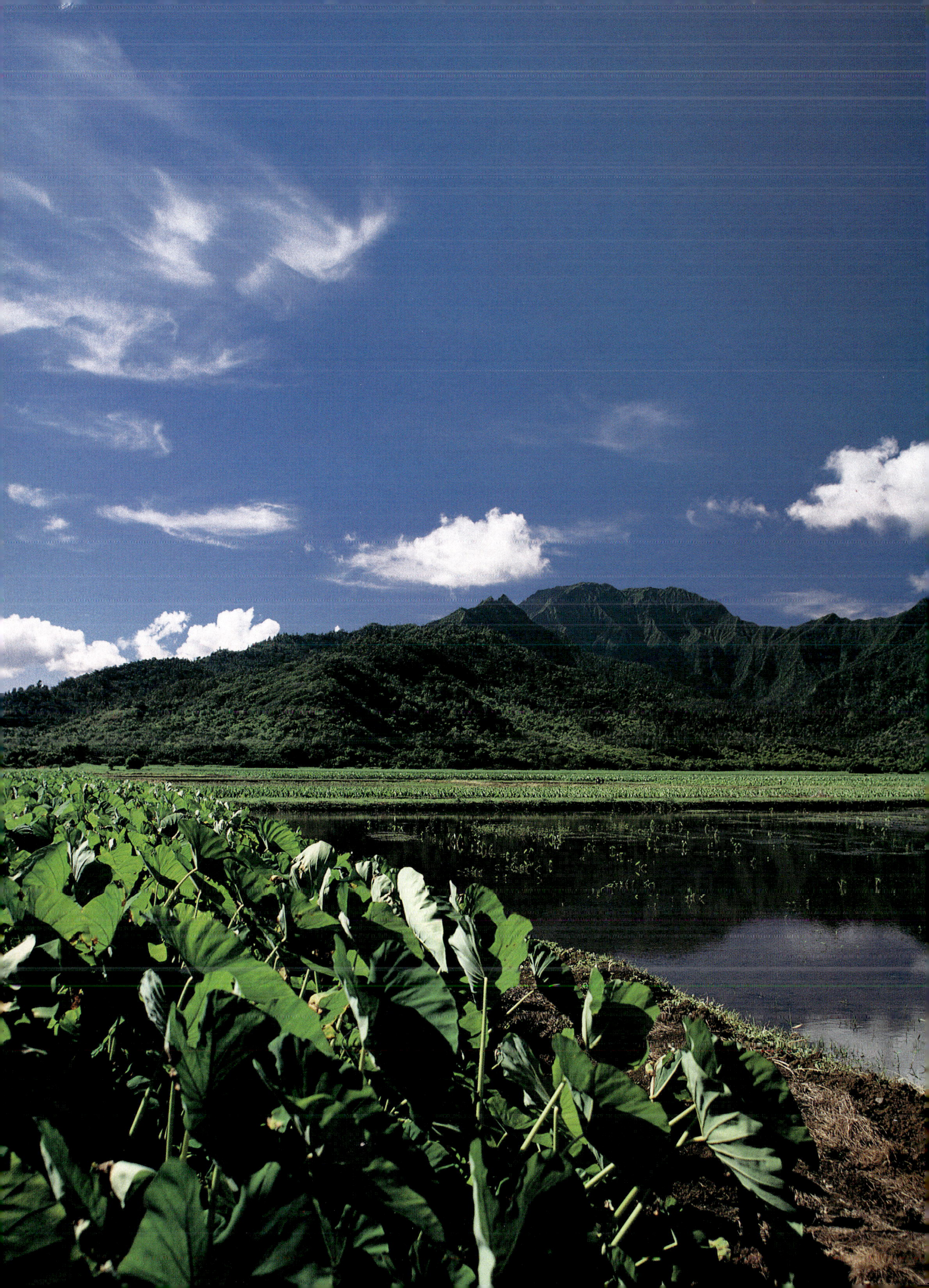

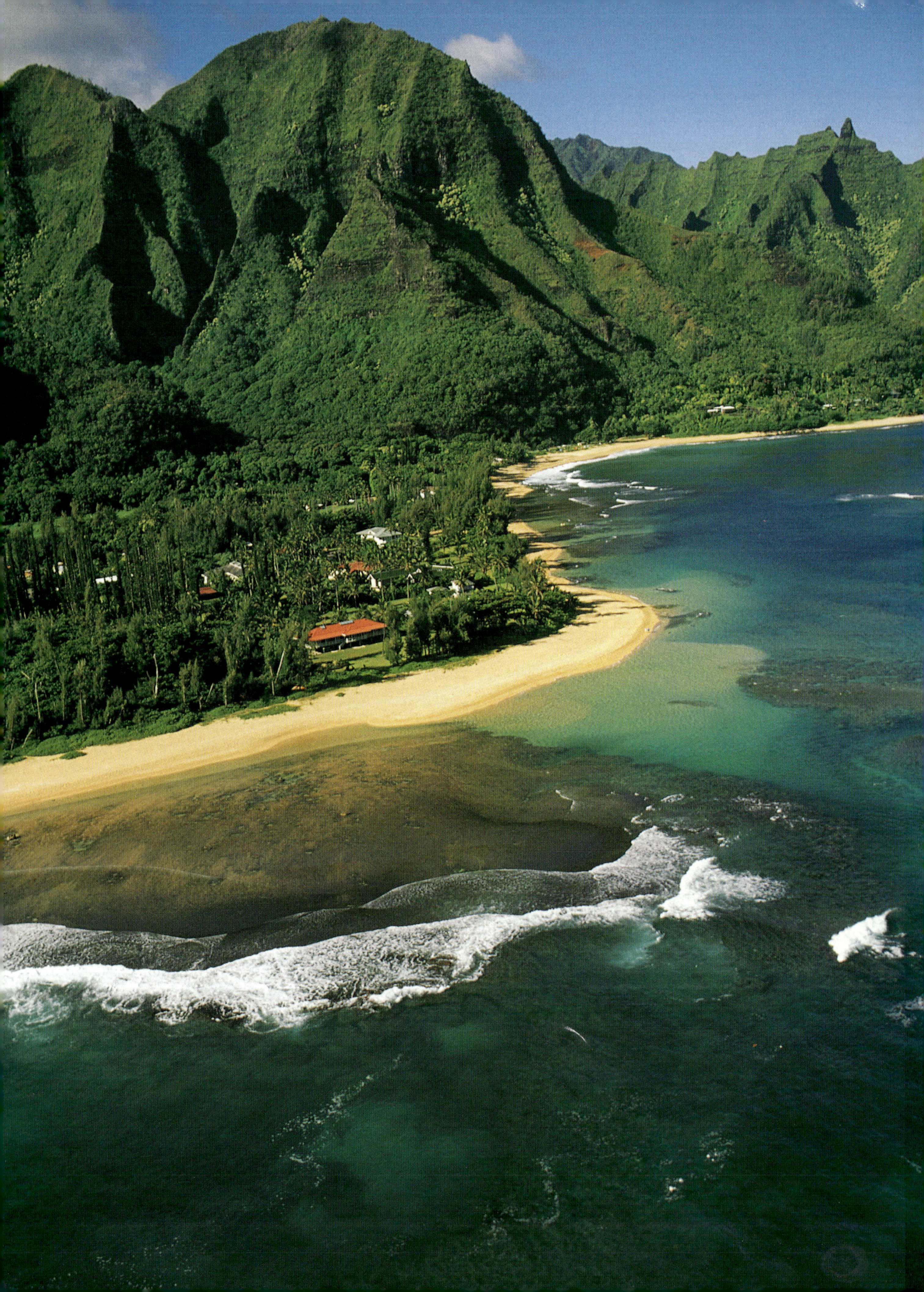

◁ The towering Waialeale volcanic ridge rises four thousand feet above the coastline of Hanalei. Because of its damp climate, this peaceful, quiet side of the island is lush with tropical vegetation.
▽ Poipu Beach glows with warm color in the late afternoon light. Located along the sunny south coast of Kauai, Poipu is a series of beaches with condominiums and hotels that face its shoreline.

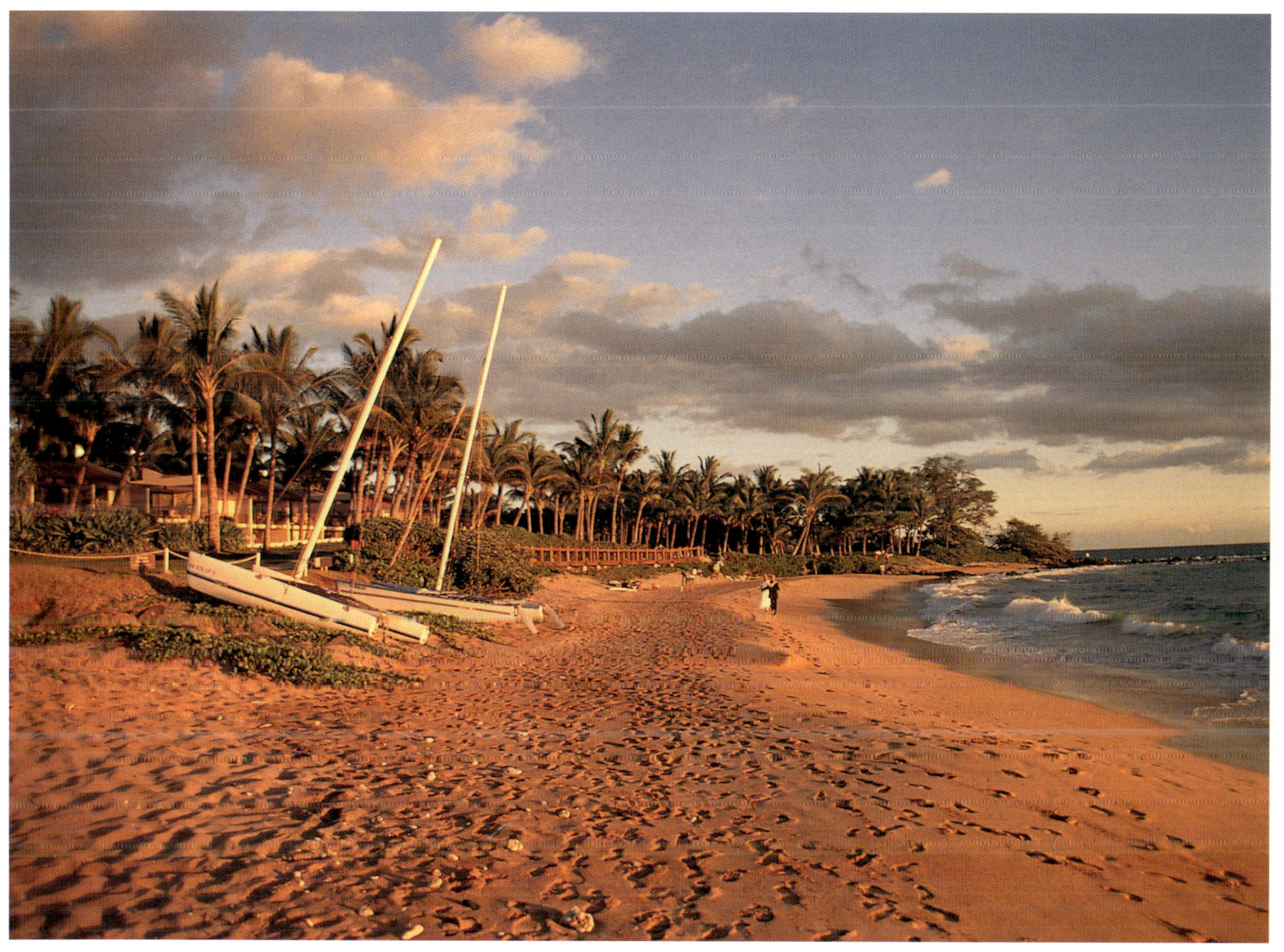

BACK COVER: The Kohala coast appears to be a barren lava flow, but it is dotted with some of the world's most beautiful and extravagant resorts. Incredible golf courses, world-class restaurants, astonishing architecture, and rare natural beauty keep many tourists here for their entire visit to Hawaii. ▽ A fire dancer at Oahu's Polynesian Cultural Center symbolizes the strength and beauty of the islands. As with all things Hawaiian, it is both the beginning and the ending of a perpetually maturing culture and spirit. *Aloha.*

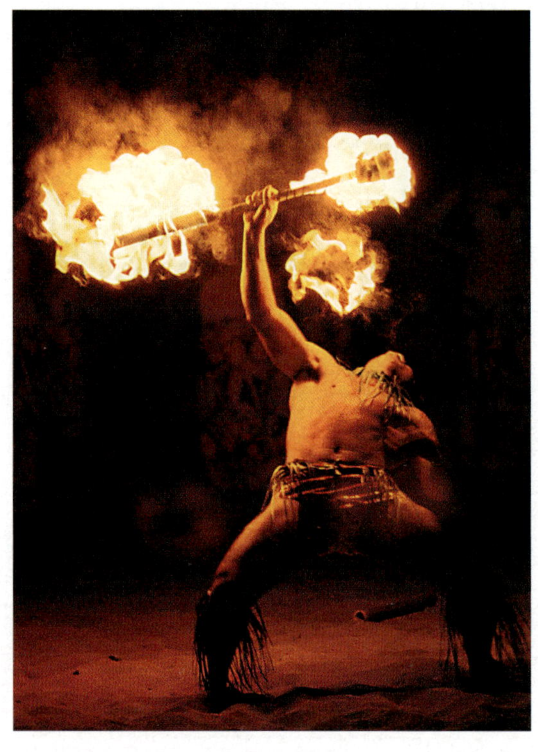